PREDICTIVE ANALYSIS AND THE THEORY OF CONSEQUENCE
BY ANDY ALLWOOD

BROWN
DOG
BOOKS

CONTENTS

This book also contains information of a historical nature, which may be of educational value; there is some threat of mild violence, some strong language used to emphasise a point, adult and childish humour, mild suspense and no political correctness whatsoever.

Acknowledgements		6
preface		7
Chapter 1	An introduction into my mind (be afraid, be very afraid)	11
Chapter 2	The tools you need to be a good predictive analyst and understand the theory of consequence	13
Chapter 3	Predictive analysis. A first step to cognitive understanding through a simple story	22
Chapter 4	The theory of consequence and how to use it to stop shit from happening	29
Chapter 5	The FWIT ("fuckwit"). An explanation, buckle up!	43
Chapter 6	ATTACKERS, DEFENDERS, CANNON FODDER	47
Chapter 7	Moving forward, what can we do to make the world a better place using predictive analysis and consequence theory?	50
Chapter 8	COVID-19: how predictive analysis and consequence theory helped me get through lockdown and beyond	56

Chapter 9	The royal family, revealing the second guardian in my lifetime	67
Chapter 10	……….	69
Chapter 11	Destin, be proud of the fallen	70
Chapter 12	Predictive analysis the theory of consequence and not all politicians are fwits or believers in the nanny state.	75
Chapter 13	But some are	82
Chapter 14	THE COVID WAR in the beginning	88
Chapter 15	Ok this time. What does the future hold for predictive analysis and the theory of consequence?	90
Chapter 16	part 2 Covid war	93
Chapter 17	……….	95
Chapter 18	Just saying, before you read the last chapter I wrote this some time ago read on you will see the relevance it has no chapter as it is an insert	96
Chapter 19	This is the last page	119

ACKNOWLEDGEMENTS

This book is dedicated to a number of individuals who have most influenced me in my life.

Firstly, my long-suffering third wife Sue, whom I love dearly and who puts up with all my eccentricities.

Nelson Mandela, in my view the greatest human being in history, who understood the theory of consequence, and was a guardian of this planet. I know he would not approve of this, but if anyone disputes his guardianship, they need to be bitch-slapped!

Margaret Thatcher. Love her or hate her, she was the greatest leader of this country in my lifetime and an excellent predictive analyst. She understood the theory of consequence, made this small country great again, and gave back power to the union membership and unions as a whole. (I feel a need to bitch-slap coming on, just read and you will understand.)

Grandad Smith, my maternal grandfather, who was the most interesting man I have ever had the pleasure of knowing and the best predictive analyst in his field as a scholar of form.

Additionally, a shout out to all the care workers (defenders) in the world that dedicate their lives to ensure those that they protect don't get eaten!

PREFACE

Before I start, here is an important announcement.

These two ailments 1 Covid 19 is a virus 2 malaria a bacterial infection please read on

Ok masks: I do get it, but stop it, will you? Making them compulsory is just foolish. Before we go any further, I don't want anyone to break the law. That is also just stupid and unhelpful. However, now is the time for the individual to take a step? Make a fuss gently, write letters, not emails, and don't ring. Be rational, the facts are there: this book will provide you with the relevant information you will need.

Let me explain and make things clear. DO NOT BREAK ANY LAWS: it's not big and it's not clever!

The best and most comfortable mask you can have if you want to avoid gum disease and CO_2 rebreathing (in my opinion and based on my training) is the bandana; a triangle of cloth tied behind the back of the head. Your glasses may still mist up but there is little you can do about that. If you want to help in the war effort, print on the front of your bandana four rules: DON'T TOUCH YOUR FACE, WASH YOUR HANDS, DON'T SHARE SURFACES and DON'T BE A SPACE INVADER. Alternatively, you could print it on a T-shirt!

We are at war, make no mistake. Follow these four rules. It's a small step, people, and if you are a teenager wash your hands before and after you squeeze that zit.

You want to join the battle? Don't say I don't give solutions – I am a defender. If you break the law now, please don't breed: the world can do without your spawn! "I don't care, in my opinion, that type of person can't read anyway." Get engaged. WE ARE AT WAR, THE ENEMY IS UNSEEN, SHOWS NO MERCY AND WILL NEVER SURRENDER. BE PREPARED FOR THE LONG HAUL.

Within this book I make reference to the Japanese. The Japanese are honourable, hard-working people and probably the most law-abiding in the world along with the Swiss, although in the past their leaders have made some very bad calls. The references I have made are based on this data and are not meant to be disrespectful to their people or culture. The past is the past: we can all learn by ours and others' mistakes. Know your history and learn to forgive like Nelson Mandela did with those who imprisoned him and supported apartheid.

There are also many references in the first chapters of this book to defenders, attackers and cannon fodder. There is a whole chapter dedicated to them, so have faith that I will get to the point, read on, get to it in turn, and don't jump. You need to learn to walk first.

The word 'fuck' is also used in this book, not in a sexual or derogatory way, but it is intended to be a powerful means of expression. If you have seen the film *Four Weddings and a Funeral*, then you will know what I mean. I am not trying to make you wince; it is, as I have said, a powerful word and, when used in context, can drive a point home, a bit like a mallet on a tent peg! Be open-minded.

I have never bitch-slapped anyone in my entire life, although I have seen it done, and when done properly it is a strong and degrading means of punishment, right up there with hanging. My reference to it is only metaphorical.

Now, on the matter of language: Danny, one of my proofreaders, is a practising Christian. Whilst she enjoyed the book and understood the bad language used in context and for effect, she expressed concern that I could lose some of my potential readers if I didn't tone things down a bit. I really respect Danny. Both my wife Sue and I think the world of her and her family, so whilst I have left some of it in, I have made changes. Ladies and gentlemen, may I introduce two words to the English language to hopefully maintain the intended impact, still get my message across to as wide an audience as possible, and hopefully not offend those I wish to protect?

1 **Fwit** (a fuckwit): a mammal with a predisposition to undertake a range of actions from just plain silly to the completely outrageous. This stupidity may be vocal or physical and may sometimes amuse them and others. Equally, it can anger and upset, and in the extreme cases result in serious injury or death. **Fwits** being the collective plural. Fwit covers all genders and species.

2 **Mif** (a mind-fuck): when something occurs which is seen, heard or felt, or is said, confusing and bending the mind. This may range from the mildly thought-provoking, to disturbing, extremely worrying and tormenting. A mif can affect all forms of organic life, sometimes resulting in death or injury caused by panic. **Mifs** being the collective plural.

Sometimes I will leave fuckwit in rather than the smoother and more pleasant fwit, as this provides more impact where emotion and anger need to be more pronounced.

Finally, before we start, I was a full-time fireman for 31 years so this may give you some insight into where I am coming from when you are reading some of the sections.

YOU HAVE BEEN WARNED.

I now feel you have been warned enough, but I am a defender, so unlike the Japanese I did not want to bomb you and declare war at the same time. So, take a deep breath, buckle up and enjoy the ride as I drive fast, so keep up (ARE THE PIGS READY IN THE BACK?)

If you burn this book after buying it and all the warnings I have given, what can I say except thank you, my work here is done and I got paid?

CHAPTER 1

AN INTRODUCTION INTO MY MIND
(BE AFRAID, BE VERY AFRAID)

When man first stepped out onto this earth armed with objective reasoning, he knew that everything on the planet was either out there to kill him or eat him or both, and not necessarily in that order! The survivors and successful Homo sapiens were the ones that could predictively analyse, realise the theory of consequence; kill the motherfucker before it killed him and eat it for the nutritional value and contribute to the survival of the fittest.

Life was simple back then.

Well? you may now ask. What the hell is predictive analysis and please explain the theory of consequence? Hmmm, have patience, we will get there and you will, I hope, enjoy the journey and be enlightened into my world. I hope to enable you to improve your existence and that of the world, or if nothing else, make you laugh, cry or leave you with the feeling you need to bitch-slap that fwit next door!

Please don't resort to the latter. Hopefully, after reading this, you will understand the theory of consequence, predictively analyse the situation and, with the knowledge of sound reasoning, seek a more subtle revenge.

All learning needs to provide one or more of the following things; it can be fun, necessary (to stop you getting killed or eaten or both, and not necessarily in that order) or to enlighten the mind. The knowledge gained may help you to protect your own, to earn money or enable you to make the world a better place. The list is endless.

Personally, I am going for the fun and to make the world a better place approach.

To support my desire to educate myself and others, I spend approximately two hours a day looking at news feeds from around the world. I gather lots of information, storing some of it for later reference. Every so often I come across some fantastic stories and facts that disappear moments after publication. They have been removed because of an objection and a desire to not upset other nations. I wish I had recorded some of the more epic ones, the pinnacle of which was the run into Baghdad Airport, Second Gulf War covered by Fox News and live-streamed, warts and all. I had to keep shutting my mouth to stop the flies from choking me. The Fox reporters were very brave men and the US military – well, hats off, guys, what can I say? Epic. FOX, please send me an unedited copy of the coverage. Unlike the coverage of 9/11 and the Twin Towers which in parts, because of my profession, left me both in tears and gobsmacked, the Fox Baghdad coverage was not seen by that many people.

Moving on…

CHAPTER 2

THE TOOLS YOU NEED TO BE A GOOD PREDICTIVE ANALYST AND UNDERSTAND THE THEORY OF CONSEQUENCE

These are quotes from other people or things I have come to believe myself which I believe will help you become a good predictive analyst and understand the theory of consequence:

- If something is too good to be true, it probably is
- Learn to walk before you run. After all, face planting is painful, so you would be advised to watch a baby learning to become mobile; it hurts and they learn quickly. If they don't, you may well have identified a budding fwit, so take care how you deal with that information
- A predawn ditherer would have been killed and eaten and not necessarily in that order, enhancing the homo sapiens gene pool. Don't dither. In these times, the gene pool is being diluted by the survival of ditherers (pipe down, defenders! Not everyone needs saving – I know, I know, it's in your DNA)
- The first answer is probably right
- Decisive action will normally be the best course of action (or at least, the thing will have to kill you before it eats you, so at least you won't get eaten alive)
- The herd will never make the right choice in time to avoid being killed and eaten, so at the very least, make sure you are the fastest in the herd

- Do not let emotion cloud your judgment: it will nearly always end badly for someone or everyone
- You must learn to forgive, but that does not mean you don't learn your lesson, so don't stick your hand in the fire, it will burn, wear a condom, and don't get into bed with the Devil or his spawn.
- Learn to see the wood for the trees or, even better, the blade of grass for the rolling savannah plains.
- If you are a sheep going into negotiations with a lion and a wolf, go heavily armed if you want to realise your ambitions
- Random acts of kindness are a little step to making the world a better place
- Passing it forward is another little step to making the world a better place and it always touches my heart
- Career politicians should never be trusted (they should be killed and eaten and not necessarily in that order, or feed them to pigs as they eat anything and my bet is a career politician will taste bitter)
- Checks and balances are the foundations of a good society and lessen the chances of you getting killed and eaten
- Those that believe in the nanny state are normally career politicians and you know what I think of them (eaten slowly and made to suffer for their stupidity, yehhhh – remember hungry pigs)
- Freedom of speech is an important part of checks and balances and must be protected, or the weak will land up being eaten, probably alive
- Decisions by committee will very likely not go well for the herd: they nearly always will get eaten

This is beginning to sound like I am in favour of killing and eating

Predictive analysis and the theory of consequence

people which is not the case. I have found that good, graphic, humorous writing will get your point across without boring the hell out of the reader, who will instead remember what they have read. As a result, I believe it will be another small step into making the world a better place.

I could have stopped here but bollocks to that! Let's continue.

- Be a believer in OVERKILL, it will save lives or at least make the enemy regret their decision to be a fwit and vow to never make the same mistake again or even surrender earlier. History can also be remembered by others.
- Everyone has been a fwit at least once in their life sadly; some make a career out of it (see the chapter on fuckwits)
- Necessity is the mother of all inventions
- Stress is the result of sound reasoning having a fight against the strong urge to bitch-slap the fwit before you
- Stupid decisions have one thing in common; they are made with emotion, a lack of predictive analysis, no use of consequence theory and a lack of common sense (don't bitch-slap the fwit before you, just don't vote for them: "simples").
- When in danger, breathe deeply and walk away backwards facing your enemy or wild animal so you don't get eaten. Unless of course you are heavily armed, prepared for the fight, want to defeat the mother and right is on your side. But remember, don't make it personal as that is an emotional decision and yes, you guessed it, could land up with you getting eaten
- A bet to win is a sucker's bet. Always bet each way (a direct quote from Grandpa Smith)
- All sound thinkers sometimes wonder whether "natural selection, would it be a good thing?" and have that stressful moment where they want to outlaw warning stickers. We

have all been there. No, don't lie: YOU HAVE!
- There is no such thing as an expert, as no one can be an expert. Anyone claiming to be is a fool and not to be trusted. It is a pompous claim made by people who are up their own arses and, you guessed it, should be bitch-slapped every time they open their mouths. There are, however, specialists in their field of knowledge. They can be the best in that field, if other people say they are because they have provided proof through proven true predictions, based on their analysis.
- "Experts" are fwits, just guessing with their fingers crossed behind their backs, wondering if they have said enough to get the fee promised.
- The world would be a much better place if the term "experts" was a term of extreme ridicule. "Ow look, here come the experts," said with ridicule and disdain. "My, aren't you the expert?" Just saying that is a put-down in itself. Go on, try it! See! Told you. No matter how you say it, it's a put-down. (Lmao, now you need to stop, the whole plane is looking at you, you were saying it out loud.)
- The smallest act can result in extreme ramifications (I will be giving examples of this when explaining the theory of consequence)
  - A smile and a nod is a small step
  - Giving up your place in a queue is a small step
  - Letting out the driver waiting at a junction, small step
  - Saying thank you to a stranger when they make a small step, small step
  - Saying good morning or evening with a smile, small step
  - Returning small step with a 'thankyou' or 'you are welcome', larger step

Predictive analysis and the theory of consequence

- Making someone feel good about themselves and benevolent towards you can be the difference between life or death. It does not mean you don't come heavily armed, just take your sunglasses off so they can see your eyes and know the smile is true. Yes, your eyes are part of a good smile.
- Do not make the facts try and fit what you want to believe, 'experts' are doing that all the time (cook them slowly: when the screaming stops, feed them to your dogs) (no, not pigs if feeding them to pigs; make sure they are raw and alive, kicking and screaming)
- Stick to the plan, but always be flexible and ready to accept change if needed
- Rolling around life with your head up your arse will get you eaten, but hey, go for it, natural selection will take place anyway

Another small note here; sometimes I may come across a bit harsh but I am trying to educate people into making small steps. If the fwit is running around with his head up his arse but pulls out this book, reads it and starts making small steps, then my work here is done. He is no longer a fwit, he is a valued member of society and making a difference. Whoop! Whoop! We are going to change the world.

- He who hesitates is lost (unless he is a very, very lucky bastard, is so rich it won't matter (unlikely) or their partner is a defender, loves them very much and saves them). I will explain my definition of defender later.
- Power corrupts; absolute power corrupts absolutely
- Always read the instructions (men are not good at this but women on the whole are, that's why more men get eaten than women)
- In litigation when apportioning blame there is now a feeling

there should be three verdicts: guilty, not guilty, and **they were a dumb arse**. Perhaps instead of putting warning labels on products, there should be a helpline number so if you are not sure of something or considering using a product to do something that it is not intended for, you could ring?
- Case in point: little wet dog and a microwave. If you don't know the story you are justified in recoiling in horror (sometimes you just can't stop, stupid).
- A good predictive analyst does not necessarily need to understand consequence theory, but they must know their history
- The herd is easy to predict and control, even more so now with modern tech and communications. This is why it is so important to have checks and balances like good unions, oversight committees, backbench committees, internal affairs, auditors, complaints departments, boards of enquiry, a civil service, a free press, independent advice bureaux. These are all part of most modern countries and governments, basically to make sure that those in power don't get corrupted, control the herd and obtain absolute power. The last man to obtain absolute power of any country was of course Hitler, and we all know the cost to the world of that one.
- Individuals can always surprise.
- How do we stop racism? There is a great quote from Morgan Freeman:

  "Stop talking about it.
  I'm going to stop calling you a white man
  I'm going to ask you to stop calling me a black man."

Great man. Small steps people, small steps. The only difference between Morgan and Mandela, I am sure, is that Morgan, like myself, has been tempted to bitch-slap that fuckwit in front of him.

Predictive analysis and the theory of consequence

I will ask him if I ever get the privilege to sit down, buy him a drink and have a chat.

- All lives matter
- History is written by the winners
- Extremists are not terrorists, but all terrorists are extremists
- Extremists are promoted to terrorists as soon as they use any sort of violence.
- Even the good will sometimes (unintentionally or not) stray to the dark side. Forgiveness then is paramount
- If you want good things to happen it's up to you to make it happen; don't think there are 'make good things happen' fairies. Only you will get it done. Small steps, people, but you do need to start putting one foot before the other.
- Hindsight should never be used to try and lay blame for a disaster. Take ten years and then look back without emotion, find out what went wrong and make sure it does not happen again.
- In times of disaster, those not in power love to manipulate the herd to stampede it into those in power, to gain control of the herd.
- The first act of any dictator when they come into power is to disarm its population: FACT!
- Small steps can quite often have the snowball effect
- Being nice is easy, being civil a little harder, being respectful harder still, but each will nearly always pay dividends. Being a fwit is easy, being nasty and cruel even easier. Being a believer in the nanny state? Well, people, being one of those will nearly always land up with you getting eaten.
- Empires are created by attackers on the backs of cannon fodder and kept by defenders

- As you age you begin to appreciate just waking up in the morning
- 'Hey, where are the tools?' They are in your head, use them wisely to understand. You may not agree with a lot of what you are about to read but at least it will make you think.
- The young are unstoppable, feel invincible and believe they can change the world. The old have survived, battered and bruised from changing the world but are now qualified to be an elder. The elder looks down from his spot overlooking his people admiring the young fwit messing about with his friends, all trying to outdo each other. He smiles and thinks, "Should I say something?" He ponders all the scenarios, smiles and finally thinks to himself, "Nah, he needs to learn this lesson himself, like I did when I was his age. The only thing he will hurt is his pride, when everyone is laughing if the stick gets stuck up his arse."

ONE LAST THING. Never gamble more than you can afford to lose. This applies to everything in life, not just about betting and is a major point to remember when you are considering consequence theory and predictive analyses. Will you be able to put food on the table till your next payday? If she finds out will she leave you? If you put your head into the lion's mouth will it eat it? Saying yes when asked, "Does my bum look big in this?" Should I really be this drunk when packing my parachute?

Sometimes defenders know the risks and that the odds are stacked against them. The two brothers, both firemen, one downstairs, looks at his brother as he enters the lift. He turns and the haunted look says it all. He turns back and goes into the lift with his men. The look said: Goodbye, see you on the other side. They were travelling to their death as this was the 9/11 Twin Towers

Predictive analysis and the theory of consequence

but THEY WENT ANYWAY AS THAT'S WHAT DEFENDERS DO.

The documentary that was made about 9/11 was made with real footage as it happened: it was compelling and will haunt me till the end of my life: just writing about it now has brought me to tears, lest we forget the fallen. Rest in peace to all taken that day, may your gods be with you.

I need a tea now.

It does take time to forgive but forgive we must, or the hate just continues. Finding a way will always be difficult and hard to pursue. Learn from one of the world's guardians and ask yourself, would Nelson M approve? When you see him smile and nod his head to say yes, the world will just become a better place.

CHAPTER 3

PREDICTIVE ANALYSIS. A FIRST STEP TO COGNITIVE UNDER-
STANDING THROUGH A SIMPLE STORY

My grandfather on my mother's side was a First World War veteran. Because of his skills, rather than being put into the trenches he was assigned to the Flying Corps as a technician. This was done in the hope that he would be saved from the carnage, and his skills would better serve his country in the war and after in the resulting peace.

He did survive but there was a cost. One evening he was assigned to get on a motorbike and take some dispatches to the front, which he did. On his way an enemy artillery barrage rained down, catching my grandfather and blowing him off the motorbike, throwing him into a large shell hole. Both of his legs were shattered and he suffered other horrific injuries. By rights he should have died instantly and any ordinary man would have, but he was strong, driven and focused. He was not going to get eaten. Three days later, still conscious and very much alive, he was discovered and taken to the nearest field hospital where gangrene had set in and both of his legs had to be amputated.

He survived, but the war for him was over.

I am one of four grandchildren. I have an older sister and brother and a younger sister, and our grandparents gave us all what we would call now some real quality time as we grew up.

Now the one thing that I learnt about my grandfather was

that he was a self-taught predictive analyst. Every week, without fail for as long as I can remember, my grandparents would come for Sunday roast and my grandfather would secretively give my mother an envelope. In it was always money. One day when I saw this, I asked my mother what was in the envelope. She told me, but asked me to keep it a secret as she did not want anyone to know, as it would embarrass my grandfather. I loved my grandfather very much, so the secret was safe and it stayed a secret.

My grandfather's one real interest in life besides the grandkids was horse racing. He ate, slept and dreamt horses. He had all the daily papers, including all the dedicated horse racing papers. If it was not on the television, it was on the radio. Now you are going to instantly assume he was a gambler. How wrong you are: successful gamblers merely dabble in the art of predictive analysis. He did bet on the horses, yes, but there was no emotional involvement. Winning was not important, although he did, consistently, and to provide a little extra help to his family. His love was analysing all the data, selecting doubles, trebles and sometimes quadruple accumulators, placing 6 pence to a shilling (in later years 50 pence new money) each way and watching the race on television or listening to the radio. He never bet on races that he could not see or hear. I was to discover that he had accounts with all the bookies in the area, to whom he would ring in his bets and once a month would go in and clear his account (collect his winnings). It was never a lot of money as he knew if he got greedy all his accounts would be blacklisted and there would be no more betting.

It was not about the money; that was coincidental. Instead it was his love of making predictions and getting it right, all down to analysis of race results, breeding, previous owners and trainers, how the horses looked in the paddock, whether the owners and trainers were there and what the jockeys were doing before the off. It wasn't just the horses he was betting on, it was about every horse that was racing on any given day: the weather, the placings the odds, every single snippet of information and he remembered it all. I would be sitting with him as a child and then as a young adult, fascinated at how focused he was and the wealth of information he had. If he wanted to, he could have been a very rich man, but no, it was his love of predictive analysis that drove him. I knew all this because he loved to talk to me about it as he knew how interested I was. When I reached the age of 18, he needed me to go into the bookies due to his disability, to collect his winnings every month. All the bookies were fond of my grandfather: he was a well-liked and a respected man. They would put the money in the envelope, sometimes up to £500 tax-paid, and I would take it home and give it to my mother who would, in turn, invest it into long-term savings to provide for the family and give herself a good standard of living. Lmao, if my father had known, bless him, he would have been pissed but that's another story.

That is just one form of predictive analysis and is as close as you can get it in its purest form. Coincidentally my grandfather loved Royal Ascot we all went every year whilst his health permitted. He always said about it, "Predictive rules change at Royal Ascot, because everyone wants to win". He loved Royal Ascot.

Now I have the ability to do the same thing and for a few years after my grandfather's death, I used the knowledge I had gained to make a small amount of money from gambling but it was too much like hard work and I was more interested in my long-term future. At the age of 19 I had already planned my retirement. At the age of 50 I wanted to own my own home, retire and be able to play without breaking any laws or getting eaten, and to make a difference, not in one big way but by my actions and small steps. I have so far had a very successful life. I am proud to say I have saved many lives, made big and small differences to many others, and achieved most of my goals. I am now 65, have been retired for over 15 years and I own my own home. I have no regrets: how could I? I would change nothing, as I am very happy and proud of my achievements and family.

People have always asked me before and since I retired, "What you are going to do?" I smile and answer, "Play."

I went one step further than my grandfather, although I didn't specialise. I pick up on all sorts of small insignificant information, log it and put it together with other information to come to conclusions that other normal people have not seen. At first I used it to better myself and protect my family, friends and others, just with small steps. Despite two divorces, children and what life throws at you, I achieved my main life's goals and stayed friends with both of my exes, although my second wife sadly lost her fight with throat cancer five years ago.

Damn, that went a bit dark there – hey, life is real so move on! Life will always get better (up till the point where you get eaten and we are all going to get eaten). Take a deep breath, smile (very important small step), get up off your sorry arse and change your life. The only person who has an invested interest in you, is you. Fuck it, it's harsh but true. No matter how much help you give a loser they will always be a loser until they realise that fundamental point that they need to get up off their arse and start helping themselves. Don't give up on a loser, though: yes, they will need to be bitch-slapped a few times metaphorically speaking, but a lot of the time you can make a difference and it is a small step that means that an ex-loser goes on to help others and make the world a better place. Small steps.

I know I am an acquired taste. I do not suffer fools gladly, but despite this, I have been respected for being good at my job and hobbies. Those in my care, even though they may not like me as a person, knew that they were safe and I would not let them get eaten. Call it professional pride, I am a defender.

I do not get things right all the time (if I did, I would be an 'expert fwit know it all' and have been eaten). I do make the wrong call: I am only human, but never when it really matters and normally only when it involves emotion. Hey, I have been married three times! I am very good at crisis management, do not get panicked and whilst I have been bitten a few times, so far never been eaten.

I have always used predictive analysis to make choices in how to achieve my goals, so I will try to explain it simply.

The process of easy decision-making:
1. Remember, your first answer is normally right
2. Make sure emotion is not influencing your first answer
3. Act decisively

You will not always get it right but this is not an exact science: metaphorically, if the alarm goes off, 'leave the fucking building'. Leave the herd to get eaten, but be calm and helpful. Smile and don't look worried as you really don't want the herd to panic and land up with yourself or the herd getting eaten.

MAKING MORE IMPORTANT DECISIONS:
Rules 1 and 2 are a start. Ignore rule 3 for the moment.
1. Gather all the available information
2. Sort the wheat from the chaff, remember rule 2
3. Consider what has happened in the past in similar situations (know your history)

Predictive analysis and the theory of consequence

4. Will your decision be fit for purpose and achieve your goal?
5. Is there a likelihood of you getting eaten? (Too late already, you have been eaten as you have dithered and not realised that you were actually considering an easy decision. The herd can rest easy, natural selection has worked in their favour.)
6. If rule 8 does not apply, move on to rule 3: act decisively. If you have analysed things correctly shit should not happen. If it does, then it was not just an important decision, it was a very important decision

VERY IMPORTANT DECISIONS:
Start with rules 1 and 2, ignore rule 3 for the moment.
1. Gather all the available intel
2. Ask specialists for information, Google it. A couple of warnings: only ask a friend if you have complete trust in their knowledge of the subject, because they may well have a biased view or say what they believe you want to hear. Also when considering asking an individual, know their agendas.
3. Consider what has happened in the past. Know your history and consider whether any decision is going to be affected by predictable human behaviour.
4. Sort the wheat from the chaff
5. Is your decision fit for purpose and will it achieve your goal?
6. Does it have flexibility and be adjustable if circumstances change?
7. If the answers to questions 8 and 9 are yes, then you have reached the point where you consult your loved ones and you will need to have all the answers to all their questions

and concerns. It's important you listen and take in what they say because they may well come up with something your analysis did not reveal thus, affecting your assessment against 8 or 9 or both. Thankfully they have saved you from getting eaten. Remember rule 2.

If everyone is happy and you all understand the theory of consequence, then apply rule 3 and act decisively. If you have analysed things correctly, shit should not happen. If they don't understand the theory of consequence at this point, then make sure they do. It would be better if they had read this book before you involve them in decision, to lessen the shock and take the general pressure off them.

One last thing (I tend to use the principle of P.S. a lot): Decisions by committee will very likely not go well for the herd, they nearly always will get eaten. When an important decision needs to be made, then regard the committee as your family and do 1 to 9 first. Then, when the time comes, invoke 10. Our modern politicians need to take a note of this process and use it. You only need to know your history to know I am right.

And we have now reached the point where I need to talk about the theory of consequence, and come back to predictive analysis once I have covered the basics.

CHAPTER 4

THE THEORY OF CONSEQUENCE AND HOW TO USE IT TO STOP SHIT FROM HAPPENING

Ok, the theory of consequence is easy to explain: every action you take, every decision you make and act on, affects everything. From getting out of bed in the morning, saying good morning with a smile, to the miserable dickwad next door or your best friend. Sending a memo with "you are sacked" or "you are promoted", to inventing the atom bomb and letting the dog out last thing.

Case in point: "nah I am too tired", so you don't let the dog out. It shits on the floor. When you come downstairs in the morning you slip up on said shit. Break your leg, land up in hospital, can't get to the interview and lose that important promotion. The fwit that gets the job screws everything up, the firm goes into receivership and when you come out of hospital you have no job. Your wife has left you because she only stayed with you for the money and hated that dog, you have no home, no life, but hey, you kept the dog. He looks up at you with love in its eyes ------ (**don't:** you were a fwit, it's not his fault, he's still a puppy and he was busting and literally shit does happen).

If you have not seen the 1947 film starring James Stewart, *It's a Wonderful Life*, then you should. It is the most gut-wrenching, roller coaster but uplifting film ever produced. You could stop reading this book now, get it online and watch it, but you must watch it to the end. Then come back to this book, or watch it later: it is a true classic. It will help in your understanding of consequence.

Ok now, even minor actions can make a difference. As I keep saying, small steps. Roll that into predictive analysis and you have a powerful tool to make a difference to help change the world for the good. Yes, bad people could use it to do bad shit and they do, but fundamentally human beings only really like being good with the occasional bit of naughtiness. Bad people, however, are lazy or get voted out or land up in prison, or all of the above, so the good will always win.

When life was simple: kill, eat, survive, reproduce, things were easy. Man became stronger, had less intelligence than woman, all they had to do was provide, protect and fuck. Women, on the other hand, had to become more resistant, resilient, intelligent, bear the pain of having children, feed and protect her young, keep her mate happy by sometimes having to suck it up, as well as bear the stress of resisting not to bitch-slap the fwit. So, the man kept sucking up the hardship of providing and protecting her and her young to further the species. She would probably kill him when someone better came along, although nowadays she just divorces the sucker. Hey, guys don't blame me, it's better than being eaten; mmm for some maybe not.

How the male of the species has stayed on top for all this time I really don't know but we have; things are changing. Now, guys, stop shitting your pants, women have much more compassion than men: we are lucky bastards. If they lose that feeling of compassion, though, it will be carnage, as most men will get eaten. Only the lucky ones will survive and be used to further the female species before getting eaten. Hey, look at spiders, the writing is on the wall, guys, what can I say?

Predictive analysis and the theory of consequence

Please don't get me wrong, I regard feminists as extremists, maybe much more low-level than say Isis, vegans or politicians that want to vote for the nanny state. They are much further down the extremist food chain. Girls, you are better than that, statistics don't lie, you are still more intelligent than men overall, plus you are more compassionate and physically more resistant. Use predictive analysis, understand the theory of consequence, and take smaller steps: you will get there.

WHAT? Hey, guys, I don't want to be involved in the carnage and I really don't want to be eaten, suck it up!

Ok, ok. I will explain the vegan comment; again it's about consequences. All the vegans I have known and hear speak about their lifestyle choice always seem to want to force it down everyone's throat, figuratively speaking – no pun intended (hey, I lie, there was!). Vegetarians don't seem to do this and I understand their lifestyle choice, and enjoy cooking for them because you have to learn to be more creative. However, I love meat too much and as a type 1 diabetic, it's a much cheaper and easier way to sustain a healthy diet so I can live longer. Sorry, that is a fact and if you try and tell me I am wrong, I will bitch-slap you till you cry, don't fucking test me.

To go further, here are some simple facts that are all about the theory of consequence. This planet needs a diverse ecosystem. We need all animals and most definitely we need to be more organic, which is one very important step, and not a small one, to save the planet. It makes sense to eat some animals and use their natural products which are sustainable. Yes, we do eat too much meat and we can do something about that, but meat and fish protein are necessary food groups to sustaining a balanced diet, especially in the young.

Don't – my hand is getting ready, shut it (no, really, I am happy to discuss).

Ok, all you eco-warriors charging, screaming at me, desperate to silence my blasphemy, I give you the island of Madeira in the Atlantic Ocean. I have warned you, as a wise sheep I have come heavily armed to this negotiation table so back off, motherfuckers, you are very close to being killed and fed to the dogs. I don't want to eat you, you disgust me. What, they are still alive? (READY THE PIGS.)

The art of negotiation, that's another thing that people who are good at predictive analysis and understand the theory of consequence excel at. (I have been divorced twice, never used a solicitor, stayed friends with both my ex-wives, and helped many others to do the same.)

So, getting back to the reality of consequence, for many years the US government State Department has been warning the Californians that they need to eradicate the invasive tree species, the Australian eucalyptus. The state is run by the Democrats and has been for many years (interesting fact here: the founders of the Ku Klux Klan were Democrats), have pooh-poohed and given the US Federal government the finger, as they seemed to like the growing silver landscape that was building. Oh dear, a perfect storm was brewing. Unlike the natural vegetation which is slow-growing, the eucalyptus is fast-growing, recovers quickly from fires, loves drought conditions (in fact loves all conditions), drops a great deal of highly flammable foliage, and the tree itself is highly flammable.

We have seen in the last two years the consequence of their stupidity and willingness to try and blame it on global warming. Now, time to be harsh, please cover your ears, children.

GET UP OFF YOUR ARSES, YOU FWITS, ERADICATE THE EUCALYPTUS. IF YOU DON'T IT WILL GET MUCH WORSE, YOU

DUMB BUNCH OF FWITS. DO IT BEFORE MORE PEOPLE DIE. I am sure the US government has said the same thing but with a less dramatic tone.

Sorry about that, but I have a very low tolerance for stupid and you will notice, I did not say eaten (for once). It needed to get serious so I ask for your forgiveness. I love America and California especially. My favourite baseball team are the San Francisco Giants, I've seen them play and win whilst sitting in the bleachers. Fantastic game. They won in the last innings, bottom of the ninth, third pitch, home run hit: the crowd went nuts including my wife, who does not like baseball. You had to have been there, epic.

Another small note here. Yes, I do swear a lot. Hey, I am not writing a children's book and you were warned at the beginning. Yes, I could cut it out but I am trying to emphasise a point. I am not an evangelist, I know my imperfections but I am trying to get the point across to everyone. Two of my proofreaders are Christians and vegetarians and dear friends. I know they will forgive me and understand the context, and on reading this I know they will smile and agree. If I am wrong, I am sure they won't eat me (hey, it's an each way bet: Christians and vegetarians).

Small note here: they did not eat me, but I did take on-board what Danny said, so I have toned it down, as I said in the header. I do want to appeal to a wider audience and sometimes I need sensible people like her to give me a figurative bitch-slap to cool me down.

I am also going to give you another similar example of consequence, involving fire.

Australia this time:

The Aboriginal people of Australia are a highly intelligent and evolved race and undoubtedly the true masters of predictive analysis in their field, survival. They are also the rightful owners of that continent. They have repeatedly warned the government, over decades, of the dangers of not having controlled burning, which they have been doing for at least centuries, but more like thousands of years, to stimulate growth and renewal, making fire breaks and to stop houses from burning down. They warned that if they ignored the warning, with the right conditions, the whole continent would burn. This year conditions were another perfect storm and the continent burnt. One news company covered a story with an interview with an Aboriginal elder who basically said, "We told you so." The story went out, much to the horror of the Australian government who scrambled to cover it up and quash any other interviews involving the subject of controlled burning. Then by manipulation of the world's press with its willingness to march to the drum of global warming, managed to hide the truth. Again, I am not disputing that the human race is affecting this planet in many ways. We are, but we need to get rid of emotion and stop trying to get the facts to fit the 'expert' assumptions. Use predictive analysis, realise the theory of consequence, be decisive AND CLEAR THIS SHIT UP. Ow stop it, I am not trying to win any votes, I am trying to make people think and change the world.

Now, as individuals, we can make a big difference. As I said right at the beginning, it's about small steps and the snowball effect. First take your rubbish home. If you see rubbish and it is safe to do so, pick it up, put it in a bin, or even better recycle. If you see someone drop something, pick it up, call out to them and say with a smile, "Excuse me, I think you dropped this." Do not be rude; if they ignore you do not say anything, pop it into a bin, keep that smile going but be smug, you have earned it and walk away; others will see this and change their mind about 'not putting that food wrapper in a bin' and in the bin it will go. Unless they are complete fwits, then all I can say is hopefully natural selection will decide to eat them before they breed.

Now remember, I have no time for stupidity, so don't be shocked, and yes, I did just say that.

Education starts at home. People have forgotten this and for a lot of people due to the COVID-19 pandemic, this is now a reality. This has made most parents realise what teachers and the education system does and how valuable they are, but it also has given a lot of families some real quality time together. It is going to be interesting to see how good an effect it will have on the country; I am sure overall it will and I am using history, facts now present and predictive analysis with the theory of consequence to say this. Small steps, people.

Small steps: read with your child at bedtime. Start at an early age, they will have a good night's sleep, you will be relaxed and less stressed, and you will be calm. Although horror stories are not a good idea, I am talking to the goths here. I ended up reading to my two kids *The Lord of the Rings* because first, we had used all the books in the school library, and second, because it's my favourite book of all time and I have read it countless times. Third, it is a fantasy, a damn good read and gives the reader an insight into human behaviour. They were enthralled. I love reading out loud: I do all the voices and it took about eight months. Epic, you have to live that one.

Hats off to Peter Jackson, director, writer and producer of *The Lord of the Rings* film trilogy. It was a very good example of predictive analysis and provides an insight into the theory of consequence. It is an absolute masterpiece from conception, start to finish and the marketing. I have the director's cut extended addition with how it was made. Epic. Every so often, we have an LOTR day. Start at 6–7 am breakfast, 1st part – lunch, 2nd part – dinner, 3rd part finish 8–9 pm, on wide-screen HD: never get bored of it. Jackson's production really did the trilogy justice, but I can understand Christopher Lee's point regarding the cuts he made. I am sure you have forgiven him, CL: Tolkien would have been proud.

Ok, back to the task in hand. This one is a double-edged sword. It shows what a nation can do with motivation and a collective belief in what their leader and his 'experts' do is right. In 1958 Chairman Mao, the leader of the Chinese people, wanted to feed his people, stop the persistent food shortages and subsequent famines. He came up with the plan to eradicate sparrows, rats, flies and mosquitoes. He saw the figures that showed killing all the sparrows would free up 60 million tons of grain which was true: there were about 1.5 billion sparrows and they did eat a lot of grain.

The population was mobilised and power to the people, they quickly achieved their goal. (Now we come to that moment: I am not going to swear this time because it was done with the best intentions, but they did not follow the basic rules of predictive analysis. They were swayed by emotion and making the facts fit their belief that it was the right thing to do.)

Grain was only a very small part of the sparrow's diet. Other pests were their main food source. On the eradication of the sparrows, the resulting explosion in the pest population was catastrophic. The voracious and rife insect feeding frenzy caused widespread deforestation. The misuse of poisons and pesticides all contributed to the Great Chinese Famine (1958–61), in which an estimated 30 million people died of starvation.

Whilst this is a horrific thing to happen, hopefully we can learn by our own or others' mistakes and move on.

These three main stories are all true. I do not have a photographic memory so I might have missed out a few minor details, but they all show how the lack of proper predictive analysis and lack of understanding of the theory of consequence can result in SHIT HAPPENING.

Ok, that is the negative side of not obeying the rules of consequence and using predictive analysis to make the right call, now we have the positive.

Imagine this: if Adolf Hitler had been dropped as a baby by the midwife and he had died, there would have been no Second World War, the Jewish people would still not have a home and would still be being persecuted and killed just for breathing, the Communists would probably be in charge, man would not have reached the moon, no atom bomb, no internet or computers. Pollution levels would be at the point where global warming was now a reality and WE ARE ALL GOING TO DIE. Fuck, we really dodged a bullet there, people. Glad now she didn't drop him?

Ok, ok, take five.

Moving on…

The American Constitution and the Bill of Rights 1787–91. The formation of the Bank of England in 1694.

Without a doubt these two events are the most important things that have saved humanity in modern times. Even though one is over 200 the other 300 years old, they are very relevant today and the only two reasons we have not all been eaten and evil rules the world (fuck me, you're thinking, that's a pretty bold statement!). Let me explain. I am willing to discuss, but think about it first.

THE AMERICAN CONSTITUTION AND THE BILL OF RIGHTS

The British, after the formation of the Bank of England, became the most ruthless and powerful nation with the largest empire on the planet ever. The only check on us was the French, but even they succumbed after the Battle of Trafalgar on 21 October 1805. (This should be our nation's main holiday like the Americans' 4 July but no one sees it, although Nelson did get a statue.) The only thing to save us from being complete dickwads was and still is democracy. We had checks and balances, sound and decisive leadership, and, on the whole, we had a conscience and weren't bad people.

We were still ruthless fuckers and were determined, in our own self-belief, to own the whole of the New World, the Southern Hemisphere and the Asian subcontinent, and rule it with an iron fist for 'their own good', because we knew best and for the money of course.

Well, did I mention we were ruthless and so were the French? Ok, back to the story. The American continent was the new frontier, the New World, a place where we could transport all our minor criminals as it was cheaper than imprisoning them and we needed them to help colonise the New World. In fact, every country in Europe was awash with people who wanted to make a new life for themselves and saw America, quite rightly, as a very good option, so they flooded to the Americas.

Now, we were not alone in realising the potential and wealth in the North American continent. The French had designs on it, too, but both of us did not take into account (theory of consequence) the type of people that were now populating the continent. The people of what is now the East Coast states of the United States (not Canada, as we had that part of North America sewn up and under our complete control) were made up of fiercely independent, driven, well-educated, strong, unafraid of a fight people, and, as the British were to find out, very ruthless motherfuckers, too. Well, I do not have the time to bore you with that story; suffice to say it is

Predictive analysis and the theory of consequence

a very well-documented struggle by both the winners and for once the losers. If you like history and have the time, study it, because for once you can get an insight to both sides of the story, it's fascinating. The Americans gained independence on 4 July 1776. The French did help but only because they wanted to stop the British and pick up the spoils. That did not go well for them, because the French were hated just as much as the British and could not take on a very strong now independent United States of America.

So now we come to the crux of the story. The leaders of the independence movement were very intelligent men and knew the theory of consequence and what would happen if they did not come up with something that could safeguard their fledgling country, assure the independence of the individual states, and protect the people from themselves and from becoming a dictatorship, to keep it a free country, develop and prosper. After a few years the Constitution 1787, then the Bill of Rights 1791, became enshrined in American law and made the United States the country it is today. Many have tried to change it, but the authors were all very good predictive analysts and followed all the rules of very important decisions and completely understood the theory of consequence. Even the second amendment (the Second Amendment (Amendment II) to the United States Constitution **protects the individual right to keep and bear arms**. It was ratified on 15 December 1791 as part of the Bill of Rights). This is probably the most contentious element of the Constitution and Bill of Rights relevant to today. If they lose that, which I am sure they won't, GOD HELP US ALL.

May I remind all you liberal, nanny state-loving, budding dictators:

The first thing a dictator does is disarm the population when they come to power. FACT.

Power corrupts; absolute power corrupts absolutely.

And, may I remind you most of us are sheep living amongst wolves and lions, metaphorically speaking. Also, may I remind you that I am British, born in England and, according to DNA testing, of Anglo-Saxon stock. I am not American. No relations are either. We have some of the most restrictive gun laws in the world, but for now we can still own and shoot guns both for target shooting and hunting. Hopefully the Liberal/Labour, nanny state-loving, budding dictators don't finally get their way, and ban all shooting: this country will be all the worse for it if they do.

Checks and balances; smile and respect your fellow human beings.

Fun fact: in the nanny state of California, the busiest shops when COVID struck were, yep you guessed it, gun shops, and theirs were also the busiest in the whole of the United States. God bless America and I mean that.

Now we come to the formation of the Bank of England (1694)

The wolves and lions were at the door of this great country, the government was broke, the British Navy were the only thing between us the wolves and lions, but needed massive investment. We were on the brink of being eaten alive, shit was about to happen. Damn, fuck, how bad, very, very fucking BAD! I now think you get my point, even though I might be understating it.

A group of investors who truly loved their country and did not fancy being eaten alive even more, approached the government with the proposal of forming a private bank and, with their money, fund the British Navy and more. These were very rich, clever men who not only did their predictive analysis but also, like the forefathers of America, really understood the theory of consequence. The British government bit their arms off and the rest is history. We fucking kicked arse.

Ok, a bit of a simple explanation but if you want more, then there is a BBC documentary released on 26 June 2019. A very interesting programme which I would recommend to anyone who likes that sort of thing. I have seen it twice. Love it. Epic.

Now, I am more than willing to discuss my earlier statement that without doubt, these two events are the most important things to save humanity in modern times. Even though they are over 300 years old, they are very relevant today and the only reasons we have not all been eaten and evil rules the world ("Really?" you are thinking. "That's a pretty bold statement"). It would be fun to discuss (I won't bitch-slap you, I promise) because I love a good discussion and it would mean you are realising something. Small steps.

Last note on this. We should have a group of statues of the original founders in Parliament Square and a national holiday in their honour. Just saying.

Finally, the Bank of England has been the model of all central banks throughout the world. Damn, I am proud to be British.

See, more P.S. than you can shake a stick at!

So, I think I may have made you realise we need to think about the small things so, if shit goes wrong, you can stop and fix it quicker and possibly even stop it happening. This pandemic has done just that for a lot of people but not so much for our leaders because they are mostly defenders (have patience, I am just about to explain).

If we all slow down just a little and think through simple things as well (oops, I am driving too fast, don't shout, smile, even though you don't want to) as the more complicated, you will make your life flow better, you will live longer with less stress, but don't overthink it. Emotion is a good thing most of the time, just don't make decisions solely on emotion, it won't end well. The one thing that has happened with the COVID-19 pandemic is just that (enlightenment) for many. Small steps, people.

We in the Western world and others have got used to being safe and getting everything we want. We expect our leaders to get it right all the time. Now, I am going to be nice but I am going to shout. If you start to cry and feel hard-done-by then consider not having children, as you are doing the human race and this country a disservice. GROW UP, YOU BUNCH OF LILY-LIVERED FWITS. WE ARE AT WAR, IN FACT THE WHOLE WORLD IS. BE THANKFUL YOU HAVE FOOD ON YOUR PLATE AND CLOTHES ON YOUR BACK. DO YOUR BIT AND STOP THINKING YOU ARE SPECIAL, OUR LEADERS ARE DOING THEIR BEST. HELP THEM AND STOP COMPLAINING. DAMN CHILD, YOU REALLY DESERVE A SLAP. We are at war, don't touch your face, wash your hands, do not share surfaces and don't be a space invader.

I thought that this had to be said, as I am finding that people regard it as all over when it has only just started. It is now Saturday 22 August 2020, we have been at war since the beginning of January 2020, although the first bombs started to be dropped towards the end of 2019.

The next big offensive will start in either October or November 2020. COVID-19 and its allies will ramp it up: make no mistake, they mean to kill as many as they can. You will only have yourselves to blame, if you don't arm yourself with the weapons provided, DTYF, WYH, DNSS AND DBASI, and it all goes horribly wrong for you. I hope there are enough defenders around to save even the fwits, as all lives matter.

Moving on...

CHAPTER 5

THE FWIT ("FUCKWIT"). AN EXPLANATION, BUCKLE UP!

Now, as I said at the beginning, the word 'fuck' is used a lot in this book, it's unfortunate that it has been degraded into slang over the centuries, but I hope that you can look past its slang use and connotations and realise its true power as a word of expression to drag it back into the light.

A further definition: fwits, they are genderless and most mammals can have their fwit moments. Anyone that has owned a Retriever will agree with me. A fwit human being laughs at their own jokes when no one else does, does stupid things without a thought of consequence, and does not realise they could hurt someone and/or themselves. It is a condition that can be treated, but, like COVID-19, is deadly for some.

Ok, you are thinking, they are just stupid. No, you are wrong, everyone in the world has at times been a fwit or had fwit tendencies. Maybe not Nelson Mandela or Queen Elizabeth II, but the good and clever are not immune from this condition (Harry, SS uniform, party as a case in point).

Yep, sorry, Morgan, but you and I have both been fwits. Smile and nod when we sit down and have that drink and I will tell you mine if you tell me yours.

Being a fwit is a condition, which in some is manifested in only mild symptoms. You will know that you have had it because the guilt will stay with you forever. It lessens, though, with age: you will only wake up occasionally in a cold sweat, reliving the realisation of that fwit moment. Also, there are far fewer female fwits than male. The human female has more compassion and intelligence than men. Sorry, guys: fact.

It attacks the young and in savvier cases, parents will shake their heads in shame, get divorced because the father will not believe that this came from his loins, his partner must have had an affair. He is an attacker, please forgive him or he is a former reformed fwit and racked with guilt at what he has spawned. As I said, please forgive him, he is a good man, just misguided.

As humans age, the condition seems to lesson and stop being life-threatening; most of the time they do recover on their own without treatment.

It is a condition that attackers very rarely contract but does affect cannon fodder and defenders alike.

Attackers can get a similar condition called "nasty fwits", which will ultimately consume the host who will be eaten from the inside out, if we are all lucky. Those around them will be feeling helpless and afraid that they will be taken down with them. Four fine examples of these are Tony Blair, Idi Amin, Hitler, and to a much lesser extent Hillary Clinton. She, thankfully for the world, was not as clever as the other three.

Stop it, these are my views only, but you know I am right. If you don't, then please, let's discuss and I will gladly tell you why it's not your fault.

So, we know that this condition is out there but what can we do about it? Sorry, but it's in the DNA of all mammals. I give you the Retriever and dolphins. We cannot immunise against it, but we can lessen its effect in humans in two ways:

1. Good parenting
2. Punishment. This is one of those times of important or very important decisions in your life as it must be proportionate to the crime. Any punishment should be made and carried out with no emotion. Once you use emotion then you will make a bad call: haven't we all been there as parents? Initially, silence and the Paddington bear stare. Most of the time even for adults this will be enough, avoiding the ultimate penalty (capital punishment), which on the whole I don't agree with. Once a person has paid the ultimate price they cannot be brought back. Not a good call, so no emotion.

    I even don't agree with it for those who say, "I am an expert, of course." Well, they could have said it under duress like a defender would, to save the innocent. As you have gathered, there are varying degrees of fwit, from the silly, bad and harmful, to very nasty. I said from the start, attackers are not normally known for being just fwits, they are generally very nasty ones.

Now, dedicated vegans are unlikely to be fwits (no, they are not, it's a lifestyle choice which some like myself think is a bad choice). But respect to them for being committed to their beliefs, they make people think and, ultimately, we do need extremists as they are one of humanity's checks and balances.

No, I said dedicated vegans. Not the ones that do it just because they think it's a good idea then give up. They are fwits and definitely those who do it to get a shag, they are sex pests as well, preying on vulnerable vegans. (We have already covered this one.) I did not say this earlier as I did not want you to think I was trying to suck up or feel guilty, I did warn you I don't do PC. Maybe the vegans that have not burnt this book by now take it as it is, realise that I am just trying to make a point; they carry on trying to change the world and make it a better place. Checks and balances, small steps.

3. Comedians (it's complicated) are not fwits. Well, a few are but the modern good comedians are not, they just pretend, or have moments of it, but then admit it and make a valuable contribution to humanity. The best example of this is Russell Brand. Lmao, he really has surpassed himself many times in the past: he is a master of his art as a fwit but as he gets older he gets wiser and more thought-provoking. He remains a fwit but you have to love him. The world needs people like him. Checks and balances, small steps. I will cover more in my next book if this one gets published, which could be doubtful with the number of people I am beginning to upset. Arghhh, fuck it!

Ok, I think this subject is covered for the moment, I do hope it has given you some insight and good karma.

CHAPTER 6

ATTACKERS, DEFENDERS, CANNON FODDER

This is a generalisation on categorising the three types of human beings. Gender has no sway on these three positions. I am not going to go into the categories of each, that's a whole book entirely, but here is a small tip to start.

Put clever and stupid cannon fodder in the same room together and leave to cook, you will land up with a room of stupid. Fact.

On seeing stupid, an attacker will normally walk past, wait for the screams, smile and be satisfied that natural selection is working in favour of furthering the species. The defender will normally wade in, even though his common sense is stressing him out (let them die, let them die), and save the fwit. Cannon fodder, well, this is a tough one, it's a hard call but suffice to say, whatever happens to the fwit will cause all the witnesses to have bad dreams (except goths). Ok, if you rubberneck you are cannon fodder or a goth (no disrespect to goths: my daughter was a goth and they do make good defenders as they mature, they are just a bit morbid). If the fwit is lucky, a cannon fodder with signal will ring for defenders, the rest will take pictures, especially if the object gets stuck up the fwit's arse.

Ok, we are only human, we are wired with basic conditions. The first two are fight or flight. In fact, these two responses govern pretty much all of the other human responses. We need all three types of humans to survive. If we are lucky enough to have a guardian in our lives (I will cover those later), then even better. Cannon fodder covers most human beings and are the most adaptable of humans. If there are not enough attackers or defenders then a cannon fodder will step up (normally unwillingly) to be either. They will nearly always make a good job of it, then drop back when no longer needed. Cannon fodder are the easiest of all to be.

In extreme circumstances it has been known for a defender to step up to be an attacker then drop back, when the situation is under control. Out of the three types, most inventors are cannon fodder, as are scientists and thinkers, the lazy, the workers, those that enjoy the party when they get there, the list is endless because most of humanity are cannon fodder. Be proud that you are. Just think before you whine and complain. There is always someone worse off than you, but they are probably far happier and better people and worth saving.

Attackers are the most aggressive: we need attackers, but they do what their definition suggests, they attack. Dictators are always attackers, most hardened criminals are attackers, explorers are attackers. Attackers don't bond well, they can be fun for a while but then get hard to control, even for a defender. My second wife was an attacker. I loved her to bits (she gave me two great kids) but God, she was hard to live with. When the hammer goes down, though, you need attackers and as attackers get eaten, cannon fodder and some defenders step up and fill the void.

Defenders: well, it goes without saying, doctors, nurses, most firefighters, those that look after the vulnerable, are all defenders. They are normally focused, hard-working, sarcastic, don't suffer fools, make very good negotiators, protect the herd and help the attackers defend the herd. If, in times of extreme need, there are no cannon fodder able to step up to be an attacker, a defender will become an attacker and will turn the tide (Winston Churchill).

If you are thinking what am I...? You are cannon fodder. Attackers and defenders will not even question, they will know. Hey, be proud of what you are: without you, we would be lost.

Guardians: in my lifetime there have been only two: one of these is of course Nelson Mandela, it goes without saying (don't, your face is still hurting from the last one, want another). The second I will cover later. Look! I did warn you about the suspense bit. (Ok, I will give you a clue: they are still alive at the time of me writing and no, it was not Maggie T, she was a defender.)

If you are a people-watcher like me, or a little bored, or want to have a bit of fun with the kids, you can play spot the human. Are they cannon fodder, attacker or defender? When you get into it as a family game, it will get quite rowdy. There will be a lot of laughing and people will give you strange looks. Try it. The rules: everyone needs to understand the three types, everyone has to agree with your assumption; there are no winners or losers it's about observation and having a bit of fun.

I will also know when I walk past a group of people and I hear them say, "He is a defender," that my book is an international bestseller and I am on my way to pick up my converted Tdi 2.5 D2 Land Rover from the airport valet parking (just saying). The war is over, we have won and everyone is making big and small steps (I am ever the optimist).

CHAPTER 7

MOVING FORWARD, WHAT CAN WE DO TO MAKE THE WORLD A BETTER PLACE USING PREDICTIVE ANALYSIS AND CONSEQUENCE THEORY?

First of all, I will say everyone has the ability to understand the theory of consequence to a certain degree. It's a natural ability but people are losing it, as the perceived need is dispersing. This is because we have all these 'experts' and advisors (fixers), telling us what we want to hear, lining their pockets with our hard-earned money whilst we have become lazy and complacent.

We don't see the need to think that maybe throwing the rock at the bear is not a wise idea because it will only make him angry and he will eat you. However, sooner or later we are going to have to kill the bear to survive otherwise we are going to starve AS NO ONE IS GOING TO THROW THE ROCK FOR US, and definitely not the 'experts': they have already all been eaten. So, we need to start thinking: bear, kill, eat, what are my options? Thus, you start your analysis and weigh up your options.

As I said, life is a lot more complicated now. Some specialise and some become jack of all trades (like me). Others just join the herd and wait to get eaten. What I want to do is try and break up the herd and avoid mass slaughter like the buffaloes following the American Civil War.

We must reject the nanny state, we need to be proactive,

don't squander your vote by not voting. If you don't like any of them make a protest vote, for Monster Raving Loonies or BNP, for example. So, when on the odd occasion one of the three main parties lose their deposit and the complete no-hoper keeps theirs or, even better, wins like the Greens in Brighton, it makes the mainstream parties sit up and consider how they are going wrong and change direction.

Consider your actions, I cannot stress the point enough: everything you do affects everything! Putting that plastic bottle in the recycling, a smile (I have done this one, moving on, small steps.) Pick your battle wisely, do the easy stuff first and get the kids engaged into the right way of thinking. Hey, look at Greta, see what she has achieved. Ok, a little bit misguided and was nearly pushed into Second Coming Prophet status, but has she offered any solutions as in line with stages 7 and 8 of very important decision-making? Who the hell thinks it's ok to scare vulnerable children and give them nightmares. Sorry, guys, who is sick?

Step back please, it's not the world leaders that are solely at fault, it's the people that voted them in, then let them get out of control, and it's everyone. We cannot solely rely on our leaders. We have to take responsibility as well and help ourselves. The first time we see there is no rubbish to clear up as the crowds leave Glastonbury Festival and events like it, we will all know that the population of the world is getting shit done. Then Greta can come back and bitch-slap the world leaders as she will be old enough by then to give them a hefty wallop and tell them, "See what we are doing now: get things done." I am sure she won't swear, as she is a good kid at heart; I blame the parents myself.

Now, let's take a closer look at some other more important issues. First, renewables and recycling. I have been interested in renewable energy and recycling since as long as I can remember. In fact, as a kid I used to earn a lot of money by collecting glass bottles and some cans, returning them and collecting the deposit. I own my own solar panels and make a good profit on them every quarter. The Greens were up in arms when it was proposed to put windmills on the Downs above Brighton, citing the destruction of the Downs' natural beauty as the reason (sorry, guys, stop being extremist hypocrites and very NIMBY). Needless to say, there are windmills now above Brighton. I love my Discovery D2 2.5-ltr Tdi Land Rover and it will probably be the last car I ever own. If I need it to, I can run it on veg oil, but with a little bit of money I will either convert it to run on electric battery or, even better, hydrogen fuel cell. The latest tech in hydrogen fuel tanks is very exciting so watch this space. Ow, I will need you to recommend this book to a friend so they buy it: make it an international bestseller so I can realise this ambition.

Moving on…

Recycling food, animal and organic waste into digesters producing gas, then either using the residue for fertiliser or compressing it into pellets and burning it in high-pressure, clean-burn furnaces to produce electric power must be an option. Wind, solar, there are loads of ideas and possibilities out there, that can be funded not only by private investment (tell me where to sign), but also by government. For me, one of the biggest mistakes our government made just recently is the cancellation of the tidal power plant in Cardiff Bay. We have the longest seafront of any other European country, which is ideally suited to tidal power. What the fuck, you complete fuckwits (sorry, this time it needed to be said in full). If ever there was a time for crowdfunding and private investment, to change this country's future forever and make us Number One in the world, this is it. Just saying, people.

Micro-farming (look it up). This is not rocket science, we all need to get on-board, be proactive, get engaged, don't be part of the herd by being lazy and not caring. It's not about the world ending because we ate one packet of crisps too many, it just makes sense.

If you want good things to happen, don't think there are 'make good things happen' fairies who will get it done. There aren't. Small steps, people, but you do need to start putting one foot before the other.

I am sorry, I have just bitch-slapped myself, I sounded like I am some extremist nut bag coming across like I am some sort of 'expert'. Damn, my face hurts!

Ok you are smiling again, thank the heavens, let's get a little light-hearted here:

The lovable old rogue was on his deathbed, surrounded by his whole, very large family. His eldest son, a priest, the black sheep of the family in his father's eyes but still very loved, leant down to his father and whispered, "Father, you must confess, you have done so many bad things." His father's eyes opened and with a clear voice and a smile on his face replied, "My son, I love you, but everything I have done was legal, I just never got caught." With that he passed, still with a smile on his face.

Lastly, now this will be contentious but is about the environment. Ok, big pictures first. No, I am not going to talk about global warming, we have done that one. I give to you: **invasive species**. Now evolution and man are in a constant battle and man's fwit nature is really screwing with the planet. Sorry, David Attenborough, no disrespect and it's not your fault, you are a fantastic naturalist and the way you are highlighting things like plastic in the oceans is outstanding and the best work for the environment and planet you have ever done.

However, YOU DID NOT FOLLOW UP, and never have, for, if there was a time for follow-up, this is it. I am guessing you would have loved to but hmmm, I will stop there. Now more than ever it's not just about highlighting the problem, it is about offering practical solutions as well. The media have to take responsibility for this now more than ever, or it affects the kids, they start having nightmares, missing school, getting angry at the wrong people and, like all protesters, don't offer sensible solutions. Now, more than ever, parents, please get involved when the kids get scared: talk about it, see what small steps you can do and watch it snowball. They will sleep at night. Get some exercise and fresh air, perhaps teach them how to sail as an incentive.

Prince Charles is a fine example to everyone. Seeing something that no one else has and has used his status to do something about it and with many other things has made it his life's work. I give you The Prince of Wales's Charitable Foundation (The Prince of Wales Charitable Foundation became The Prince of Wales Charitable Fund in 2018 when the charities were reorganised.) I am not going to spout, look it up. It is a fine example of good follow-up. You can't just go, "Look, shit is happening," and leave it at that, you have to follow up. How do we wipe its bum, how do we stop the flow, what caused the flow in the first place? This is everyone's baby, let's start looking after it. NO, DON'T FEED IT PRUNES, THEY ARE AS BAD AS FIGS.

Yes, very simplistic, as I have said before. Get everyone involved, the time is over for demonstration, media sensationalising, celebrity bandwagon-jumping, career politicians, and believers in the nanny state. We all need to begin considering our actions, start with the little bits: not bin it, recycle it. Get the kids involved, no more nightmare scenario stories, we are all sick of them. Slap the 'experts' running around saying, "The dragons are coming, the dragons are coming." They were the fwits that let them out in the first place, or got some other fwit to do the crime. SMALL STEPS.

So, here are a few things that nature and evolution might, given some time, sort out. Some I have mentioned already. I give you: the eucalyptus, American crayfish, European wild pig to America, the American grey squirrel to UK, Japanese knotweed to the world. These are just a few things that have been done. Nature does sometimes sort it out but then we forget and do it again. Example: the Romans brought the rabbit to Britain, now they are a problem but they are good to eat and along with foxes and hunters and now an increasing raptor population, which is nice to see, they present less of a problem. Then some fwit thinks, 'Oooo I like rabbit,' and takes it to Australia: hmmm like giving figs to a baby.

- Stop crying wolf
- Offer solutions
- Educate

CHAPTER 8

COVID-19: HOW PREDICTIVE ANALYSIS AND CONSEQUENCE THEORY HELPED ME GET THROUGH LOCKDOWN AND BEYOND

Well, for once, I did not see this one coming but then truly no one did. Once it started to get real and before lockdown was announced, I went into overdrive and everything kicked in.

My wife is cannon fodder and she is pessimistic but she is married to and much loved by me, a defender who is very optimistic. I am not being pompous, it's a fact. Most defenders will understand the theory of consequence and be pretty good at predictive analysis, but not all. My son is not good at either but he is a very good defender and can adapt to be an attacker. In a battle for survival, I would want him on my side. God help anyone or anything that came at us or our own: we would eat them. My daughter, too, is a defender, is very good at predictive analysis and understands the theory of consequence. I would not be too concerned if we got separated in the fight for survival as she can look after herself and her own but, like my son, with her at my side, God help any who came for us.

Before we go any further, COVID-19 attacked the whole world. It is a vicious enemy showing no mercy. Guys, this is the Third World War and we will win it, because we are human. We have made mistakes, there is no blame to be laid, as I said earlier. In ten years' time we can look back without emotion to see what we all did wrong, fix it and learn by our mistakes and be better prepared for next time (there will be a next time). We all, for a bit, ran around with our heads up our arses, some only a little whilst others still have not pulled it out.

So please, take a deep breath and laugh at yourselves and others, say yep, that was me. We still have caveman instincts battling with modern conditions and thank your God that the enemy was not a plague with no cure (the Black Death being the big killer in medieval times for that reason. Known as the plague, it is still around today but is easily cured with antibiotics) or we would have lost by now. Relax and read on.

The cannon fodder and the attackers were easy to spot at the start of the pandemic. They were the ones with all the toilet rolls in their trolleys. As time went on the cannon fodder were further differentiated with their trolleys full of toilet rolls and wearing masks. At this point, some of you are feeling embarrassed. Forget what I have just said, we were, and still are at the time of writing this book, at war. Buckle up, it's going to be a rough ride. The defenders did buy as many toilet rolls as they could but they were buying them for their friends and neighbours, who were vulnerable, who could not get out. If you are feeling smug at this point and you only gave away a few of them because you felt guilty due to the bad press, you are an attacker. I forgive you, it's what you do. If you don't feel smug you are a defender, it's what we do. If you feel ashamed don't be, you are cannon fodder, it's what you do. You see shit happening and do irrational stuff. As I said, buckle up, it's going to be a rough ride.

For me, this pandemic has been a revelation and I am absolutely fascinated by all aspects of it and it is what has inspired me to write this book. I have never had to work so hard to sort out the wheat from the chaff as there is so much chaff. All I will say is: why oh why did the World Health Organization (WHO) not take any notice of what Turkey told them about the virus and how to treat it with anti-malarial drugs? Thousands of lives worldwide would have been saved and most countries would not have had to go into lockdown. No blame, though, emotions were running very high and every country panicked. Aliens were attacking and it came from nowhere with a ferocity not seen since the Battle of the Bulge or Pearl Harbor.

Necessity is the mother of all inventions.

Now, let's all look on the bright side (of life). We are going to win. Things will get back to a new normal which will be better in many ways. First, the advances in medical science have advanced, and are advancing, at an exponential rate which will save millions of lives going forward. We have all had a taste of real fresh air and everyone wants to keep that: the only downside is that the rise in skin cancer will be nasty but inevitable unless we cover up and wear glasses to protect us from the UV light.

Thankfully, the almost evangelical crusade over global warming has been pushed back and given the world a chance to look at the big picture without emotion and try to make the facts fit into what the self-proclaimed 'experts' are saying. Gather more data please. Meanwhile, yes, something is happening to our climate, so let's all start taking small steps and encourage our government to do it as well. Fuck the rest of the world, someone has to set an example: pick up plastic rubbish and do something about plastic waste because we are all guilty of poisoning the oceans.

The concept of working from home has been around for some time now. But because of COVID-19 it has undoubtedly become

Predictive analysis and the theory of consequence

obvious that it improves productivity, and vastly improves the overall well-being of staff, they don't have the stress of travelling to work or meetings, and communicating with the modern platforms saves time and money. Increasing productivity in this way lessens the chance of the control freaks bullying staff. Less office space is needed (if you haven't moved your money out of office space development, mmm bad call), and having less traffic on the roads at peak times, with a resulting reduction in pollution, is good for the environment. The downside is you will have to buy more toilet rolls as you will be at home more.

The community spirit has been fantastic. As in all situations of adversity, human beings naturally gather and protect. I have never seen or heard so many smiles, good mornings, thankyous, you are welcomes and simple acts of kindness in my lifetime. Yes, it is small steps, just very small ones, but we are so much better for it. I myself have never felt so alive and grateful for the excitement of living through such a monumental moment in human history (although I will be pissed if I get eaten before I finish this book and get it published). What will the world be like when we have won and reflect? The possibilities are very exciting, and have you seen the clean water in places like Venice? Amazing.

The hardest thing for me has been 'don't touch your face'. Why is it, and I am sure every sensible person can relate to this, you wash your hands, go shopping halfway round the supermarket and your nose develops an itch? I hate masks, by the way, I only wear one if I have to and I will cover that in a minute. Yes, I am still a defender, it's just ow! Read on, I am not being a hypocrite, you fuckwit. Now, this itch is starting to really get to me. Having touched the shelves and products, I have to resist, only to see a moron in front of me with his mask on, is rubbing his mask because it itches like fuck.

He is picking up stuff I would like to buy, looking at it and putting it back on the shelf. At this point I really got close to the bitch-slap moment, but with my heart pounding, I said to the guy in a loud but controlled voice, "Excuse me, but could you stop doing that?!" He looked at me and said, "Sorry, what am I doing?" I took a deep breath and explained. To his credit, he was horrified with what he had done. I was really glad I did not get nasty with the guy, he did not deserve it; he took the mask off and we talked some more about the value of masks and then we both carried on shopping. There were a few similar incidents but in the end I gave up. I just shrug and think: "Cannon fodder." Now they are compulsory in shops I can spot the cannon fodder easily and that amuses me. With his whole family in tow, walking down the high street, all with matching designer face mask: he of course has to have the best because he is a smug twat. Won't be so smug when he is told: "You have gum disease." How did I get that? he will wonder but I clean my teeth and why are my kids' faces so spotty? Ok, time to cover masks now.

Before I do, I am only talking about mask-wearing among the general population, not professionals who need to wear PPE to protect themselves and those in their care.

Right, as you have gathered, I love to analyse all sorts of subjects. One of the first with COVID-19, well before lockdown, was about "What can I do to protect me and mine?" I am a defender, after all, that's what I do. The second was masks. Now, I have had to wear masks all my life in my job and in some of my hobbies, let's say I am a very well-qualified specialist in PPE, namely masks. I know the good points and the pitfalls. I kind of want to say overall they are a waste of time and leave it at that, but I can't, because those in power dictating this requirement broke rule 2, so here goes, suck it up lmao:

Predictive analysis and the theory of consequence

I think you have probably gathered by now, I am not particularly PC: did I say this was negotiation? Nah.

First: all the Asian countries wear them, yep, that's right they do, and have been for a long time. They are heavily polluting the world and rather than cleaning shit up, they wear particulate masks and don't care about the gum disease, and rebreathing CO_2. Harsh but true. Yeah, fuck 'em. Also, the Japanese obey directives, that is in their DNA but it does not mean it's right.

Every time I hear 'All the Asian countries wear them' I want to slap the fwit that said it. So called 'experts' started that because they had a vested interest in the manufacturing of face masks. Only kidding! Or am I? That, or they just get off on scaring kids and the gullible.

Second: the best advice and better than wearing masks is don't touch your face, and wash your hands. It is still very relevant now and for the future as most viruses and bacterial infections cannot penetrate the skin, they can only come in via lungs, eyes, cuts, abrasions. The ones that can penetrate the skin are normally deadly and you need full PPE, or better, to protect yourself.

Third: most masks only slow down the virus coming out for a short period of time. If you have the infection, your first breath has infected the mask and you will touch it because it will slip, make your glasses steam up, make your face itch, whatever. You will then touch it, finger shit, leave it on everything you have touched and infect all behind, you fwit. If you have the virus or even think you have it, don't come out. If you don't wash your hands before touching your mask, your fingers will transfer the virus onto the mask and then have a perfect breeding ground and be sucked in and down to your lungs.

Small note here as I got a bit heavy there. All attackers hate wearing masks and quite often will not wear them, even when pushed. There is one exception. Devout vegans who are attackers because they are extremists (I have explained this one) but are law-abiding, either because they are sickly creatures and know their immune system is compromised by their lifestyle choice (there are no poor vegans). Even though they are attackers they scare easily when not fighting for the cause. Now, nearly half the vegans in the world are really not true vegans, they have become vegans for many reasons, not as a lifestyle choice.

First, they have met a vegan, fallen in love, become vegan, got married and had a short but happy life together, unless they secretly eat meat and never get caught. The big giveaway is they have rosy, healthy cheeks; the devoted partner, however, always looks pasty and sick unless they wear loads of make-up, which is rare as most make-up has animal products in, or is tested on animals. Second, they think it's a good idea. Some stick it out for this one because they fear the piss-take they will get from their friends because they are not an attacker. But hey, it's ok, it's a good detox and when it's over you will feel better about yourself so you can just bitch-slap the piss-taking fuckwits. Now the most popular, by far, is because you want to shag one.

Now this one is really always driven by emotion and you know what I have said about emotion: it will end in tears, either for both, or for the vegan. Truly, this is where I feel sorry for the vegan. As I said, it is really a lifestyle choice, they are normally middle-class and have unwittingly been promoted to attacker from cannon fodder. So, they are human and, like all normal humans, they like to have relationships, partnerships, sex etcetera. This leaves the vegan open to the male and female sex predators as a challenge. As the predator learns very quickly, the vegans only want to partner up with another vegan. Sad but true. I know of one such relationship.

Predictive analysis and the theory of consequence

Arriving home early, the guy concerned had been for some time involved with this very pretty, young, highly sexually driven girl. As he opened the door to his flat she looked up wide-eyed with a face full of MackyD. "Fuck," she spluttered, spitting MackyD everywhere. He, on the other hand, was shocked and horrified, went ballistic, made her pack her things and threw her out. On her way out she said over her shoulder, "You should have known all along, you hypocrite, always willing for me to eat your meat and swallow." With that, she left him gobsmacked, and she laughed all the way back home to her parents.

Now, this story is true, a bit crass, yes, but there is a happy side to this: they genuinely did like each other. When the dust settled and sound reasoning crept back, they met up and came to a compromise. They became mostly vegetarian (she and the children occasionally eat meat), got married, had children, and to my knowledge are still together to date and very happy, good people.

Ok, back to masks.

Fourth: you know it's a piss-take when they say it will be fine, just make your own, you will be safe. This one gets them every time. You have just realised the pain on your forehead is the 'expert tattoo artist' with perfect spelling and spacing and a smile on their smug face with pockets full of your money, tattooing SUCKER!

Fifth: long-term use and wearing of face masks increase the humidity in your mouth which increases the build-up of bacteria and the chance of gum disease. Please Google 'gum disease'. If you have to wear a mask, take it off as soon as it is safe to do so. If your gums are not bleeding when you get on the plane, but are when you land nine hours later, claim off the airline for your medical bills.

Small note here. Before smoking was banned on commercial

airlines it was really unheard for things like colds and flu (airborne viruses) to be passed on, as the air circulation was such that you could have someone next to you smoking and hardly notice. But this costs money, so ok, let's ban smoking so we can turn the air con down. It saved millions. Hmmm, now you get on a plane with one person with a cold: yep, every vulnerable person on that plane is a potential victim. On some airlines you can almost taste the stale air in economy (yes, first-class get much cleaner air, but they pay for it). You want cheap flights, there is a health cost that comes with that.

I wonder if, like tobacco products, there should be a health warning: 'booking this cheap economy seat could increase your chance of contracting COVID-19'. I am sure Greta would not approve: she does not fly. She sailed back, did she not? She would have been safe in first-class if she needed it.

Sixth: as most medical staff will tell you, with long-term use they give you facial rashes. In some not so much, but in others quite savvier, in a teenager with acne, not good.

Seventh: rebreathing CO_2, Google it, I can't be arsed. The world is running around with its head up its backside, with our leaders acting like fwits because the herd is in control with the 'experts' at the reins hanging on doing the bucking bronco (he is doing his girlfriend from behind and just told her, "You're not as tight as your sister").

Enough, enough. Masks: waste of time. Just don't touch your face. With people you don't know, keep your distance, wash your hands, don't share surfaces with strangers or friends without wiping them down. Think day-to-day things like sharing lighters (as nine hospital medical staff of a COVID ward did on their break, with the result of one death), hugs, kisses, tables, shopping trolleys, staplers, salt and pepper pots, joints, taxi door handles, a beer bottle. You

Predictive analysis and the theory of consequence

have a brain, use it, it is not rocket science.

Whueee, sorry, I will slow down.

At the start of the pandemic in this country, Boris was under the impression that he was elected by intelligent people. He was mostly right, when making the decisions he made, though, he forgot not everyone voted for him. Just saying.

No blame, Boris, I said that right at the beginning, wait ten years and eliminate the emotion. Anyone using hindsight to lay blame, especially now, is almost committing treason. We are at war, don't be a scumbag.

I just let emotion take control for a moment there but I am going to leave that last bit in because we are all human and as I said, and I quote, "No blame, though, emotions were running very high, every country panicked. Aliens were attacking and it came from nowhere with a ferocity not seen since the Battle of the Bulge or Pearl Harbor." Guys, just ask these so-called experts, are you an expert or a specialist? If they say, "Well, I am a specialist to be fair" (and they have never done the bucking bronco with the herd), you can trust them. If they say, "I am an expert," drag them outside, whip them till they are close to death, let them fall to the ground, pour salt onto their wounds and let them live. If they say, "I am an expert of course," drag them outside and just burn them at the stake.

No, I don't like people that call themselves 'experts', surely I have made that plain by now.

--- I have had a cup of tea and feel refreshed, sorry. ---

I don't know when I will finish this book or even if it will get published, but for now, the war is still raging all over the world. I say again, we will win but everyone needs to keep fighting, doing their bit to save as many lives as possible, and I mean everyone.

Keep smiling, small steps.

I keep harping on about emotion as if I am a heartless old git. I am an old git but I cry when the sad bit comes up in a good film. My wife knows when I am because she can see my feet twitching. I always sit in a recliner, reclined, I can't watch the adverts about starvation and poverty or animal cruelty as it makes me feel helpless and sad. It's a bit irrational for a defender because they need to be stronger than that as, whilst they do need a heart, all defenders will tell you eventually there is an emotional cost of being a defender. They are stronger than cannon fodder but still, shit gets to you in the end. Most attackers, though, are on the whole heartless, ruthless people but they have to be, they are attackers and generally feel no guilt.

Ok moving on…

CHAPTER 9

THE ROYAL FAMILY, REVEALING THE SECOND GUARDIAN IN MY LIFETIME

I thought long and hard about this section in this book. I am a devout royalist and feel this should be said.

For me, I have grown up with only one monarch: Her Royal Highness, Queen Elizabeth II. As I have said, I am a lover of history and if you are a good predictive analyst, you have to be. Yes, there are many out there who don't like the royal family, and hey, I get that. Most of the dislike is driven by emotions, though, and not reasoned thinking.

Now, most of the people of this great nation and many around the world have great respect for Her Majesty. Some even have love or great affection, even though they have never met her. The BBC have done some very good recent documentaries on the royal family so I do not need to go into details. Suffice to say, Her Majesty's life, work ethic, dedication and love for her family and her great nation and the Commonwealth, put us and every other person alive on this planet to shame. That is why she, in my eyes and I am sure many others will agree, is a guardian and probably the best the world has ever seen. Also, for me, she has to be the best predictive analyst and consequence theorist in the world ever.

Now, I have watched the two Princes William and Harry grow up, make mistakes, have fun, pick outstanding partners and turn into really good men and a credit to their parents, the royal family and the nation as a whole.

They have truly shown the world they mean to protect and serve their nation and put themselves in harm's way. The government at the time of their deployment were shitting proverbial bricks and everyone who cared breathed a sigh of relief on their safe return.

William and Harry are both defenders and when the time comes will make good kings if required, but William has the potential to become, like his grandmother, a guardian, one out of a possible two that I can see in the future. The second I will talk about at the end of this book.

I have come back to put this bit in about guardians. Some of you might quite rightly say, "Was not Winston Churchill a guardian?" My answer is this: he was a man of his time, mostly defender and if you had taken in the bit about defenders stepping up to be an attacker and what would happen as a result, you will now realise this was the case of Churchill stepping up in the Second World War. Without that great man, the world would be a very dark place right now. When defenders step up to be attackers, they will turn the tide.

I was going to say more but, to be fair, there is no need. I want to get back to the funny, fun educational stuff.

CHAPTER 10

The publisher thought this chapter was a step too far. Hey, he might be right but it was either leave the politicians, donkeys, prostitutes and hamsters in or cut the whole lot. I could not make it work without them, so we will leave it till the second edition and take another look then.

CHAPTER 11

DESTIN, BE PROUD OF THE FALLEN

Just fed the dogs before I started this chapter. Anyway, lockdown brought good and bad. It meant I was not bothered by Jehovah's Witnesses, politicians of a low calibre, vegans and general fwits, but I did develop a lot of freezer space. No, I did not include Jehovah's Witnesses or fwits in the 'people who will be upset' bit on the front cover. This is because the true Jehovah would recoil in horror at reading the cover, drop the book as if it was on fire with the flames from Hell and run out of the shop screaming, being scarred for life. Or, he really is not a true believer, furtively buys the copy his mate thought was burning with the flames from Hell, in his excitement slides it in his trousers, hiding it in his underpants to keep his balls warm. Find his mate and coax him back to where they are really not welcome. Read the book, laugh his socks off, find enlightenment, fuck off home and stop bothering us at Christmas.

Well, as for fwits they are fwits. They don't know they are fwits so they will read this book, laugh their socks off, find enlightenment, start taking small steps, and help change the world.

Ok, ok, there might be a few fwits that suss on reading this book that they are fwits, and yes, they might be a bit upset but they will be too embarrassed to admit that they are fwits. They will tell all their friends how good the book is to deflect their friends from thinking they are fwits, my book becomes an international bestseller, my D2 gets the conversion, they start taking small steps and become better people, and we save the world. Ok, now take a breath.

Ow, the freezer space. No, I don't kill people, chop them up and put them in the freezer to feed the dogs. Let me explain. The attackers and cannon fodder started to panic-buy all the frozen dog food, I suppose to feed the kids with when the zombie apocalypse happened. We ran a bit short, I have five dogs, I love them to bits and had to start feeding them the good stuff, but, like all panic buying, it levelled out in the end and went back to normal. Now, every time I go into the pet food shop to the frozen meat section, I picture all these fwits crunching through dog food. It's ok, it has to be by law fit for human consumption and yes, I would cook and eat it if pushed, and the dogs love it, it's good for them, but hey, it's dog food.

Destin was a fine ridgeback, proud and watchful. The whole floor-shitting and leg-breaking incident is behind him now. He was young and he was busting. His owner really did love him. The dog kept him on the right path, was instrumental to his meeting the love of his life, who helped him develop his ideas into a very successful business empire with all the right environmental conditions to save the world.

When they bought their dream house in the country, the first thing Destin's owner did was put a dog flap in, the same make as the other one he put in the old house after the whole shit, floor, leg break debacle. First rule of consequence theory: 'a good idea is always repeatable'. Life moved on: Destin was now 15 years old, slightly deaf, occasionally wet the bed, and his owner and his wife knew the day was fast approaching that all loving owners dread when the decision has to be made. Gut-wrenching. For now, though, he slept in his bed at the bottom of theirs, dreaming nice thoughts with the occasional twitch, muffled woof and whimper.

The three men approaching the house cut the telephone wires as they knew mobile signal in this area was non-existent. It's Devon, what can you do? They climbed over the wall and approached the house.

Destin woke with a start. Now dogs do clench their arse cheeks, as all dog groomers will tell you. He, though, was not being groomed, he needed a shit. The shit, floor, leg break horror had left a very strong impression on Destin and, as every owner will tell you, ridgebacks are loyal proud dogs. A little drop of pee was one thing, shit was just no. He struggled out of bed and made his way downstairs out of the dog flap, into the garden, and started to ready himself to resume the position.

Time stopped. Destin growled and the three armed men in front of him puckered. All they could see was the Hound of the Baskervilles, all teeth and ferocity. Unluckily, though, for Destin, these armed men were no ordinary robbers (this was when pistols were banned in the UK, just before the hand-in); they had tortured, robbed and killed an old boy a few weeks earlier, not far from where a good friend of Destin's owner and wife lived, stealing some of his collection of Second World War handguns and other valuables.

They knew what was in the house and even the Hound of the Baskervilles was not going to stop them. "Fucking kill it," the leader growled. Destin launched himself, fully aware of his impending doom, and as ridgeback owners will tell you, they will back down when the lion turns and back away, BUT WHEN THEIR OWN ARE IN MORTAL DANGER, THEY WILL DIE FOR YOU. In the dog world they are true defenders.

The ensuing battle was not a fair fight but time was the key.

Destin did cause some nasty injuries and the time this gave was enough. Over 12 shots were fired but eventually, even he could not withstand six body shots, laying him to the ground, bloody and twitching in death. The three, now furious, driven men, bloody from the fight, stormed towards the house, crashing through the French windows into a lit lounge.

Destin's owner and wife woke with the noise of the battle and jumped out of bed. He realised on hearing the first shot the danger they were both in. "Call the police, stay here." He rushed to his gun cabinet, pulled out and loaded his soon-to-be-handed-in Glock that he used for practical pistol competition, rushing to the top of the dark stairway looking down into the lounge, shaking with adrenalin and fear. "The line is dead." At that moment, three angry, bloodied apparitions crashed into the lit lounge, armed and ready to kill. Destin's father recognised his friends' long-barrelled naval Luger and instantly knew his and his wife's fate.

What went down was a blur: he was standing over one dead and two seriously wounded men. Not a scratch on him or his wife; her face was ashen with tears and shock. Holding her mobile she said, "The police are coming." She had got a signal. Grief hit her like a steam train uncontrollably crashing into the buffers. "DESTIN." She rushed outside.

He stood there glazed in shock, realising the enormity of what he had done. All he could hear was the moaning of the two seriously injured men. But then the grief-ridden wail of his wife, "DESTIN'S DEAD, they killed him!" overcame the shock. With that, he did not give a damn if they lived or died, he rushed out to his wife and their now dead hairy child.

When the police arrived the first thing they saw was a man and a woman, bloody, riddled with grief and tears, both hugging between them an old ridgeback limp with death but gone with dignity and heart.

* * *

Well, come on, guys, the trip to the vets is shit. I have done it too many times. What a way to go. The two surviving villains pleaded guilty to all charges; yes, sorry, they did survive. No charges were placed on the father of Destin. Could you see a jury convicting him of any crime? The prosecution knew that. I did hear a D-Notice was put on the story so the gun lobby could not use it to keep handguns. How true that is, fuck knows. All I can say is in the end it was lucky it was not a Golden Retriever: they are cannon fodder. Save your arse? No chance. Flight response 50%, wilful 25%, eat everything 25%. It is ingrained in their DNA. Excellent family pets, though.

All because he did not let the dog out, hmmm yes, consequence theory!

CHAPTER 12

PREDICTIVE ANALYSIS THE THEORY OF CONSEQUENCE AND NOT ALL POLITICIANS ARE FWITS OR BELIEVERS IN THE NANNY STATE.

People like to believe that modern politics and democracy were born in Greece. Total hogwash, now let me explain. The hub of human civilisation proposed by most theorists and academics is the continent of Africa (I will try not to go too deep). So, man developed the tribal system. At the same time, leaders of the successful tribes would emerge, enabling more of the tribe to become cannon fodder, so allowing the tribe to grow and establish in an area, develop farming and settle. This meant that instead of an attacker leading a small band of nomads, communities formed with defenders now in charge.

Now the thing with communities is that to be successful, they need to have leadership and a governing system. Naturally, as it was safer for the male human in this environment, the older and wiser males could offer advice and insight into all matters, using predictive analysis and consequence theory. When one stood out, he would be elected by the people and the other elders as the headman, and lead the tribe. There you have the first democracy.

Now this system is still in place through Africa and other tribal-based nations, including some modern democracies where, instead of being called headman, they are called Presidents. The best two examples of this in the West are America and France. There are others but these two are the most stable in the West.

Some others, like the United Kingdom (UK), are monarchy-based democracies. Some are good, some not so much. The UK has the best monarchy-influenced democracy in the world. The Queen has no political powers but offers advice and stability to her country's Prime Minister and is an influence throughout the world. Our Queen is one of the best checks and balances the world has ever seen to date. We have been very lucky; she is held in high regard by all party leaders by remaining neutral and, like a very good village headman, in her position as the highest of all the elders has never had any challengers. This is because the nation as a whole would not react well if she was subjected to any unacceptable behaviour (I am being diplomatic here).

I could go on but it would get boring. I want to get back to the more humorous side of this book.

I am more than willing to discuss, but before you get all hot and bothered, just remember we are still tribal. We in the UK are a fine example of small and big tribes making the whole. Northern Ireland has the Catholic and the Protestant tribes. Wales has the Northern and Southern divide tribes; the south being welcoming and the northern nationalist tribe being unwelcoming to all. Scotland has all the clan tribes with the nationalist tribe now being the biggest, the leader of which is unbelievably transparent in her hypocrisy. Let me explain. She and her party were voted in because of a rise in nationalist belief. This in itself is not a bad thing; I am all for pride in my country, its people and their achievements. Americans, when they sing the national anthem in a bar, at a game or any event, sing with a hand on their heart. It is moving beyond belief, everyone is equal in that moment, tears in eyes. Moving. I have been there many times.

Predictive analysis and the theory of consequence

Getting back to the point, when you have a leader subtly trying to stir hate and nationalistic bigotry, it is not good. "Oh we don't want to be ruled by the English, what have they done for us? We can stand on our own two feet." Hmmm really? Ok, who is going to fund that? Ooohhh, ok, you want to remain in the EU, be ruled by unelected bureaucrats so you can get into spectacular debt and be bailed out like the Greeks? It did not go well for them, Sturgeon.

Yes, I am being harsh but I was witness to the hate and violence during the build-up to the last vote of independence and the aftermath of the win, inflicted towards the great and the good. However, they stood united: thank God for the strength of the true Scots as they stood up to it and voted to remain as a united country. God, love you people. I love Scotland, would live there if it was not so cold for two-thirds of the year. The people are amazing, friendly, inventive, sarcastically funny, have been the backbone of British land forces for 2.5 centuries, medical pioneers, pissheads, sometimes scary, welcoming, and just good people. Love 'em.

The one thing that is all wrong and so disrespectful is the lack of respect for the rule of a democracy that she has displayed by not accepting the decision and, like all dictators, calling for another because it's not what she wanted.

Does she not get it? She has all the power she needs: her party has the power in Scotland. Good on you, I am proud of Scotland for that. But the true Scots believe, like Mandela, what happened in the past is in the past. The Scots people are respected and admired. True Scots know that, but they also know it would not go well if they were not part of the UK. Help make the UK number one, enough of living in the past. Sturgeon, you are better than that, you are a woman, stop making the other girls wince and move on.

Now we come to England. There are many tribes, the Cornish

with their black flag with a white cross being one of the notable ones. All the English counties have their own identities, some of which are very distinct (Oh, he is a Yorkshireman). In the end, it's about identity and we should encourage that: the need to understand where you have come from is in the human DNA, it means we are not alone.

WE ARE THE PEOPLE OF EARTH, LIVING IN A HUGE UNIVERSE. (Sorry, I have just been profound not profane: don't worry, it won't happen again, I still have loads of people to upset yet.) Ok who is next?

Cameron. YES, let's go there. Here is a fine example of a politician who starts off well, has potential, holds out the olive branch to form a coalition government with Nick Clegg and the Liberal Democrats. Both leaders, good men, and if they had been equals, they could have changed the face of politics in the UK. Well, it's all there basically. Nick was not village elder material (too young) and susceptible to bad press. Damn, you were close, boy, you were close. Well, Cameron as it turned out was just a low-level defender and elder. A good elder has to be a strong defender in a modern society. A true elder would not have thrown his toys out of the pram when the country voted out (of the EU). (I had to put that one in just in case, in a hundred years' time when studying for English Lit and this book is on the reading list, it will give the students a heads-up and they might not have Googled it then. Just saying.) It was a very proud moment for me, even though I voted to stay in, power to the people. A good village elder would have picked up the baton, done what was needed, got us out of a corrupt system, changed Europe for good and made this country proud, all in under a year. No messing. He could then go to the polls, win with a large majority and make this country even greater. We

Predictive analysis and the theory of consequence

would have jumped from 5 to 1 in world standings and could then have said FIX THIS SHIT and it would have got fixed. Aah, just saying, missed opportunities and all that.

Oh, please stop it, we are one step forward from prehistoric man, one hovering step to anarchy. Please wake up, you fwits. Think before you get on your self-important high horse (Think I said, "Did I panic-buy toilet rolls or dog food?" And no, you were not buying them for your neighbours, we have done this one, you fwits.)

------------ Damn, take a deep breath.-----------

All the rotting food being thrown out in the first few weeks of lockdown proves it. We have basic fight or flight and when the herd is being ridden by the 'experts' doing the bucking bronco, all the defenders are shaking their heads, thinking, 'Where did evolution go so wrong?' Have I made my point? Good, you are not a bad person, it's in all our DNA. Those on their own were the most vulnerable, they are the ones who have paid the biggest price. Emotionally some were made stronger, some will always have nightmares but thank heavens for BBC Radio, community response, computers, and the fact that humans are basically good with only tendencies to be naughty.

What makes me proud to be British? The BBC, the United Kingdom, the Bank of England, the British military, the royal family, the NHS, BP (yes, an oil company: I might explain if I have time), our universities, our teachers (but not our education system), our quality manufacturing, innovation, the people of this great nation (even the Northern Welsh tribe), our farmers. So many things, we are a great nation, be proud SO JUST TIP BETTER, you fwits.

So, we have established: the ancient elder's system is the birthplace and model for modern politics, now let's refresh and have a moment to reflect.

Power corrupts; absolute power corrupts absolutely.

Humans are greedy: it is a basic survival instinct, don't be surprised that the fuckwits were panic buying.

Like foxes when in the chicken coop, our basic instinct is to buy all the toilet rolls (kill all the chickens), it's irrational. Yes, the only thing separating us from the fox is the fox likes killing and goes into a frenzy. Most humans will just wake in the middle of the night in a cold sweat reliving that realisation of that fwit moment. Then again, you have those who did not give a damn because they are selfish fwits.

It's important that modern society has checks and balances, not control, not the nanny state, but basic things to stop greed, abuse of power, dictators, the big, important stuff. Remember bigger is not always better, but that is for the next book.

The proud son of the Southern plantation owner brings back his new boyfriend he met whilst on his gap year in Africa. The son of a village elder, himself going to study politics in America with the intention of becoming a career politician. The proud son, the apple of his father's eye, had slight trepidation about the whole 'meet the parents' and the breaking of the news of their impending engagement. But he knew his father was not a racist, white bigot: he was better than that.

The two boys smiled at each other on the arrival at the proud son's family estate. His parents were on the porch of their home, beaming with pleasure at his safe return. His mother could not hold back her excitement: she ran forward, put her arms around both boys' necks and hugged them tight. His father came forward, too, smiling proudly, shaking his son's boyfriend's hand vigorously. "Ok son, tell us all," he said. Now, with renewed confidence he introduced his boyfriend and told his parents of their engagement. His father beamed, the smile on his face said it all, whilst his mother just squeezed them both even harder.

Then: "He is coming to America to study politics and become a politician." The smile on his father's face changed to horror, he drew out his .45 Colt, shot his wife with a headshot, then hesitated, sighed, then shot his son's boyfriend; also a headshot.

Silence. His son was shocked. "But why, Father? WHY?" Slowly his father turned, sadness on his face, "Sorry, son, but I was never sure, but it looks like she did **** that Democrat as no son of mine would have brought back his like. The world just does not need another career politician, sorry."

Ok, I did tell you I don't do PC, but the point is the elder system works and they are not always men; sometimes women step into the post and most of the time do a better job.

Now, I do have faith in the overall system: it is about checks and balances. Good politicians know this and most understand one or both of the importance of predictive analysis, and the consequences theory. The world has a habit of bringing order out of chaos. We do live in times where the extremes are highlighted by social media and used to incite the herd so the 'experts' can climb aboard. Watch your back if you see him climbing up, ready the baseball bat, smack him hard before he tries to do the bucking bronco. Use your vote wisely, question your choice, don't be fooled by the media. Do your homework, even local elections are important. Don't close the door on the canvassers, no matter which party they represent; make sure you tell them what you think and not what they want to hear. Don't, above all, shoot the messenger. They are only doing a job. (Unless they admit they want to be a career politician or an 'expert', then "READY THE PIGS".)

Now don't, I love pigs: I regard bacon as one of my five a day.

Well, I smashed through that chapter.

CHAPTER 13

BUT SOME ARE

Now and for the future, we need to understand that communication and predictive analysis, with the theory of consequence, will be key. They have to be independent like the British civil service, which Labour systematically tried to dismantle so they could be complete fwits under Blair's government. We are all paying for Blair's, then Brown's Labour government corruption, with their hired henchmen, spin doctors and advisors, bankrupting this country, stealing pension funds and selling off the gold reserves to fund their self-importance. Blaming it on the crash 2007–08–09 is what I would call a nail in the coffin year which would not have happened if Brown had not removed control of the banking system from the Bank of England. They would have spotted it long before the shit hit the fan and fixed it. Ok, ok, ok, I will calm down, but we will come back to this, for it is a fine example of not adhering to the theory of consequence and allowing greed to take over, one of the animal kingdom's worst emotions.

As a matter of fact, I was talking to a group of people in October 2006 about the sub-prime bubble which was due to burst and how I needed to get some things done before it did. I was one month too late: it crashed in March 2007. For me, I assessed it should have been April. Bummer, I was going to do a little speculating but hey, still nothing lost. When I saw the same people in May, they thanked me for my insight as they had saved themselves a shitload of money. Though, to be fair, loads of people saw it coming but emotion and disbelief bitch-slapped them too hard and they could not get their shit together to stop it. Greed is a base instinct all animals have, it is part of the fight response and as humans we have perfected and corrupted it and made it into a very bad thing. Moving on…

Man's greed knows no bounds.

When Labour came to town in 1997 with Tony at the reins of the herd, he was wondering how long to hold off doing the bucking bronco. He appointed his best mate and fall guy if shit happened, and he got caught out by selecting Gordon Brown to be his Chancellor of the Exchequer.

Labour had inherited, yet again, a sound legacy from the previous government and prepared themselves not only to ruin the country this time, but also to line their pockets and those of all their friends as well. Ow shut it, it's all on record, take me to court as I am a well-armed sheep, well up for the fight. I have right on my side and I know I will win. Revenge is a dish best served cold, so bring it on, you fuckers.

Sorry about that, I just had a moment.

What's in the past is in the past and needs to stay there but sometimes people need reminding lest they forget the fallen. We all saw the bodies coming back through Royal Wootton Bassett.

History will repeat itself, we just have to gird our loins, buckle up and prepare now.

Where was I? Oh yes, 1997, 13 years of misrule and thievery. First job of Labour was to kind of sideline the civil service (one of the checks and balances), by appointing, quite legally, their own advisors and fixers which grew and grew. In the end, when the coalition government took power, they inherited that famous note: "Dear Chief Secretary, I'm afraid there is no money. Kind regards – and good luck! Liam".

Shameless! In fact, it wasn't just a case of leaving no money, it was worse than that: they had squandered a 17-billion pound buffer, spent that and still left the country billions of pounds in debt. The first thing the coalition did was sack all those advisors, quangos, henchmen, fixers and general wasters that Labour had left behind. Now, I might be wrong here with the exact figure, but I believe it was in the region of a £62 million saving as a result. Some of these nasty fwits tried to howl in protest and it should have been punished, but all kudos to Nick and Cameron, they knew it would not be good for the country, and let it slide. Nelson M would have been proud, boys. The rest is well documented, people: austerity is Labour's fault and theirs alone. Debt is sometimes the only way you can buy your own home or see you through a bad patch, but uncontrolled debt is a downward spiral into poverty and despair. To classify the whole of the then Labour government as true scum would be wrong because there were many good members then, they were just taken in by their corrupt leadership. Sorry, just my view but I stand by it, because the evidence is there for all to see.

Now I will give credit where credit is due. On the death of Princess Diana, the royal family's first and only thought was the two young Princes William and Harry. They were, luckily, at Balmoral, away and hidden from the relentless press who loved hounding Diana and the royals. Shame on them. It was one of those times when our Queen and guardian became consumed with the protection of the two princes as all good grandparents would be. Suffice to say, The Queen was needed by her people and needed to return to London to help with the country's grief and

Predictive analysis and the theory of consequence

Blair was instrumental in that happening. The rest is history and I think is the only thing to save him from the proverbial gallows, and downgrades him from very nasty fwit to just nasty fwit. Sorry, yes, in my eye a nasty fuckwit (Second Iraq War, do you really want to go there?). No, I thought not. Whilst treading on the snake's head and watching it writhe before you skin and eat it may afford some satisfaction, let someone else step up: it is not worth it. Although snake is good to eat, so they say, never tried it. (READY THE PIGS.) Practise forgiveness and step up, people, honour Nelson M Blair, you are a lucky, lucky b******.

Now, the fall guy who had become Chancellor rubbed his hands with glee. First job, remove some of the Bank of England's control over the system.

In a nutshell: America and their central bank was modelled (as all central and world banks are modelled), on the Bank of England and its financial rules and regulations. At the end of the day, all the banks and traders had to account, and settle deals and loans, as well as carry a surplus to cover any outstanding debt and possible rogue traders. Now this was hampering some very powerful, greedy bankers in America, who somehow convinced the powers that be to relax those rules: "Trust us, how bad could it get? We are bankers, we have to be trustworthy. Please, pretty please, we could all make so much more money." Classic. The powers that be had the greatest collective fuckwit moment in modern history, relaxed the rules and the rest is history.

Well, the world is going to keep having these crashes and falls because the greedy are still in charge and the powers that be are dithering and spineless. If ever there was the time for the bear to come crashing in and feast, it is now. Just saying (READY THE PIGS).

Back to Brown-the-witless. He fluffed out his chest and told the

Bank of England that the Labour government were going to do the same. The Governor and the Bank at the time were, to put it mildly (as they were bankers), a little concerned at this turn of events. Any normal person would have been running for the hills, shouting the warning, "The dragons are coming, the dragons are coming!" The 'expert' was mounting the herd with a glint in his eye, looking forward to doing the bucking bronco, but instead of making the comment about her sister, he is going to make more of an impression and say her mother instead. It was real, it was happening.

Well, the Bank of England is not prone to panic, these are pragmatic, clever people. They saw the writing was on the wall and agreed, BUT asked that the legislation give them control of the interest rates. Brown-the-witless bit their arms off, the legislation was passed, the Conservatives shook their heads, and the rest is history. You, I and the world are paying for that folly. I mean it this time (F*****G READY THE PIGS, WILL YOU?).

Are you angry now, or at least a bit perturbed of the enormity of this one action? The lack of predictive analysis and adherence to the rules of consequence? Well, you should be. The only thing that stops Brown-the-witless from qualifying as a nasty fwit is that fools are fools and should not be classified as even fwits. They can't help being fools: he was picked to be the fall guy and he really face-planted on that one. Blair, good choice on the fall guy – no, sorry, you are still a nasty fwit.

Oh come on, I am harsh, ok? If you thought I was only kidding about what I put on the front of this book and are still reading it, good on you, small steps mean we can change the world, but stay buckled up, there is more to come. My foot is hard to the floor and we are racing.

The Bank of England's hold on the interest rates is the only light in the tunnel, it has saved us going into free fall. All I can say is: well done, the Bank of England and all who sail in her, you deserve every penny you make and a medal. Possibly a statue or two. Mmm, step too far.

Seriously, though, very, very good move. Brown-the-witless did try to take the credit, but we know the truth.

One last thing. I finished this book before the Americans went to the polls. I hope Trump gets re-elected as he did what we all needed him to do but were unwilling to say and do. The absolutely disgusting world disrespect for democracy is disregarding the fact that he won, you fwits. Shut the f**k up. Sorry, just had a moment there. He is not a corrupt career politician, he is a village elder, get over yourselves.

He has done what he said he would do. He has shown, through his actions, he is a man of integrity. He has shown he is a man of his word, unlike Obama. "If you use chemical weapons we will bomb you." He gave the Russians a warning to get out of the Syrian base, bombed and destroyed it. Assad has not used chemical weapons since. He has negotiated with the Russians and, best of all, the North Koreans and has led to talks with the South and a calming in that region. The world is a much safer place because of him: we do not need career politicians, we need village elders like him.

I do hope for all our sakes he wins a second term. It will be close, but I believe in the great and the good and the ordinary American will see through the chaff and misinformation and re-elect the right man. Good luck, matey, the world needs Trump to get another term and it will be a fantastic win for democracy if he does.

Time for the next chapter: the start of the COVID war.

CHAPTER 14

THE COVID WAR IN THE BEGINNING

At the dawn of creation, the first life was microbes. The first sentient beings were bacteria. They were the first attackers. Like humans, bacteria had attackers and defenders, although they do not have cannon fodder, as for life to grow, get strong and provide a living host for bacteria to live and prosper, life had to suck it up. Live with the fact that bacteria and viruses (one of bacteria's cousins), ruled and would kill and maim for sport and pleasure; they grew fat, lazy and complacent. Much like man did before the First World War and after the Second.

Then man arrived. Well, like all life they were not immune to the attacks from bacteria and viruses. But as time advanced and humans became more intelligent, a worrying trend started to happen: man started to cure shit. Those bacteria and viruses who were true blood brothers and still reasonably sentient realised that things could get bad for them both. So, the germ wars started and have been raging ever since. One of the greatest battles being the Black Death; the name of which a bacterium came up with, to inspire fear and panic. It did this for centuries until man invented (with the help of defender bacteria and immune system stimulants) antibiotics and vaccines.

This betrayal by the defenders infuriated the attackers in the respective camps but the defenders were fed up with the carnage and, to be fair, they hated the bad press and turned their backs on the attackers, heading to their heroes, the microbiologists, instead.

Come the 20th century, the viruses headed by the leader 'The Spaniard' (like us, they like to nickname their heroes) had a notable battle with the human race in 1919–20 with the pandemic battle called the Spanish flu. Killing millions worldwide and in the eyes of the virus leaders a spectacular victory.

But they were to pay for that victory with the development of flu vaccines. As fast as they mutated, the cleverer the humans got, and life got hard. Then the humans started to have fwit moments. Measles, tuberculosis etc were on the up, humans were getting complacent, thinking they had won the war on infectious diseases and the like. A chink in the armour had appeared, the time was right: all they needed was a COVID with teeth and a fearsome leader and the human race could be driven from this planet. Enter the Stalinists (humans named it COVID-19 after the year in which it appeared) and the most feared attacker in human history, which the COVIDs nicknamed STARLIN, arose. An all-powerful hermaphrodite killer, pink in colour, with a very strong, natural immunity amour plating and a thirst for human blood.

Starlin grew up in the heavily polluted, overcrowded human Petri dish city called Wuhan in Hubei province in China. How it originated is immaterial, the human world needs to take the Mandela approach: this a deadly enemy and recrimination only divides, this is what the viruses want.

The battle was about to begin, toilet rolls and dog food: we're heading for the front line THE COVIDS ARE COMING THE COVIDS ARE COMING and shit was about to happen.

End of part one.

CHAPTER 15

OK THIS TIME. WHAT DOES THE FUTURE HOLD FOR PREDICTIVE ANALYSIS AND THE THEORY OF CONSEQUENCE?

Well, in all seriousness, if this book is a success I hope it just makes everyone think, plan a bit better and take into account the consequences of their actions. We live at an amazing time and I am excited and grateful to be alive and it is a small step to making the world a better place for my kids, grandchildren and beyond.

For me it has never been about the money. Yes, I do want to do the conversion to my D2 Tdi Land Rover and I have been promising my wife for years I will be building a castle and what I will be putting in it for her, but hey, everyone has dreams. That's the one and only time I am going to talk about the castle in this book.

It's so much more than just money. My curse (for want of a better word) as a defender is about professional pride. We are sometimes a bit hard to live with, we like things to be right. My kids love their stepmother very much and quite often say to her in my earshot that they marvel at how she puts up with me. A touch hurtful, lmao no, only kidding. They are right but they don't realise that she is cannon fodder, pessimistic, caring, intelligent and loyal, in many ways vulnerable but in others confident. All the things a defender like myself admires and wants to protect.

But defenders do have a bad side; normally if the defender feels the person or persons in their care no longer need protecting, they easily move on. (Defenders are more likely to cheat on their partners than the other two groups.) Attackers go either way but they are attackers, they hate to lose, that's why they get eaten so easily and divorces for two attackers will get very, very messy. No, very, very fucking messy: everyone saw it coming and are unfriending you from their Facebook accounts as we speak. That messy.

For once I truly don't know what is coming. There are a few things that I know would change the world and the fortunes of this great nation first and foremost. The banking system needs to reverse the overseeing measures the central banks had before the slide into greed. We in the UK with the respect that the Bank of England has worldwide should put back the controls Brown-the-witless took away, still leaving the interest rate control as well. The American government and their central bank would follow suit and every other country would soon follow. Boris, it's clear you have the balls and the Bank of England has the will to follow it through: they want it, too. Ok yes, the greedy bankers (and there aren't that many) will squeal but you know what to do with them (BRING IN THE PIGS).

Now, did I mention this earlier tidal power? It just makes sense, let me explain.

In the modern world, everything revolves around power (no, you fwits, electricity), and renewables are a no-brainer. Ok, we could go down the nuclear route but I give you Chernobyl and Fukushima; Sod's Law dictates accidents will happen, can we really take the risk of eradiating half the country? Really, you think? Even the fwits are shaking their heads now I have told them about tidal, because they know they will be the first ones to be fed to the pink nuclear pigs if shit happens.

All joking apart, Cardiff wanted it, Wales needs it, the nation is holding its breath. Despite the many attempts to derail it in the enquiry stage, everyone in the end said yes, it's a good idea and we have the resources, the tech and an ideal willing area to build the first model. No-brainer. Government, it's up to you. WHAT THE HELL HAPPENED? EXPOSE THE FWIT PLEASE?

I keep telling you I am not PC, suck it and buckle up.

Once the ball is rolling, the technology will advance, we will be able to give free electricity to the not so well off. Cable excess into Europe, no more need for gas or oil except for the chemical industry. With availability of graphene, hydrogen fuel cell and saline batteries, the list is endless, we have limitless possibilities. With tidal power which is predictable, the only drawback being if the sun and moon decide they want to move and leave our solar system, but then we are goners anyway (no, I was only kidding, we are super-fucked anyway) if that happens.

If you want a good future, we all need people at the top who can predictively analyse and understand consequence theory. As long as we have good checks and balances, all should be well.

Well, almost. Just keep an eye on the attackers and fwits and if you see the 'expert' doing the bucking bronco with the herd, you know what to do – yep, that's right, BRING IN THE PIGS.

CHAPTER 16

PART 2 COVID WAR

In part one of the COVID war we ended with Stalin, the leader of the COVID-19 virus army (the Stalinists), rising in the Petri dish of humanity; the city of Wuhan, Hubei Province, China. Let us step back and give a little more insight to the rise of bacteria and viruses as the first true rulers of this planet. You have read part 1 so I will keep it short. For millions of years bacteria and viruses had no challenges to their rule. Then the dinosaurs arose and developed sentient tendencies and started to use their brains for more than food, F**K and reproduce.

Unlike humans, who only took thousands of years to develop brainpower, dinosaurs took millions. Why bother? Life was good and there seemed to be no need, but the alarming rate of global warming caused by overpopulation of herbivores and their methane gas output was starting to worry the carnivores, who were the brains of the outfit.

It was decided that the vegans had to be controlled or the planet was doomed: damn plant eaters, why can't they just stop farting?

Well, the carnivores knew that bacteria and viruses, being the rulers of the planet, needed to be approached to see if it was possible for them to come up with a solution to just curb the gas output by, say, 30%. Not an impossible amount: after all, they were the microbiologists and understood all the rules of mutation, and development of the species.

Well, the dinosaurs knew it would be a hard sell as most bacteria, especially the males, were a malevolent, nasty bunch of fwits, whilst viruses were just nasty fwits and had no real interest in helping anyone. Still, time was running out and a group of highly intelligent dinosaurs called the Thunberg guild (they were more of a religious cult than a guild, but good, strong evidence is just not available) approached a secret group of good bacteria (yes, there were some and still are). They were the rare female order of bacteria, much more intelligent than their male counterparts and had compassion. The records are sketchy at best, the erosion of time (millions of years) has left a lot to guesswork. But a deal was struck and many of the vegan dinosaurs turned to become omnivores to lessen the pain caused by the good bacteria making them hold onto the gas and causing that bloated feeling.

Well, it was all going well till the male bacteria, who revelled in the damp, confined heat of global warming (much like bacteria in the mouth with constant use of face masks) found out what was going on.

SHIT hit the proverbial fan and war started. It raged for millions of years with no real winners or losers. No real records have been found of this time and we can only guess at the carnage, but necessity is the mother of all invention and it is clear that the dinosaurs were winning.

OH DEAR, THE ASTEROID HIT, THE DINOSAURS WERE SUPER-F**KED ALONG WITH MOST LIFE ON THE PLANET. SHIT REALLY DOES HAPPEN.

CHAPTER 17

Like chapter 10, the publicist (whilst he laughed like a drain all the way through) said it would upset the children and give girls like Greta nightmares if I did not take the hamsters, dictators, stallions and the dead radio star out. Again, I just could not make it work, so with a heavy heart I had to give in and try to rework it before the second print.

CHAPTER 18:

JUST SAYING, BEFORE YOU READ THE LAST CHAPTER

I really do hope you have laughed half as much as I did writing this book. To fuck up the people who read the last page I have included my third adventure into serious writing which has made grown men cry and is quite an emotional piece. It has relevance to the main book to help understand consequence: it is a work of fiction but has relevance. It is a groundhog story and was written in the last few months of my service in Surrey Fire and Rescue over 16 years ago. It was written to protest about the cuts happening and due to happen in the service all over this country. What saddens me is it is still is going on. I have included everything I wrote, not just the story. I hope you enjoy that, too. It is not a comedy piece, it is written with emotion and anger. Sometimes emotion can be a driving force for good but not often. It does need to be tempered with reason, checks and balances. If you want to know about the first two then hopefully it will be covered on the first television interview I have when this becomes an international bestseller and I have converted my Tdi 2.5 D2 Land Rover. I am serious: if I say I am going to do it, it will get done.

Now did I mention that there is another budding guardian in the making when talking about the royal family? President Trump will be recognised eventually for being one of the US's very good presidents. But his daughter, on the other hand, will not only become the first female President of the US, but also be recognised as one of the very best and regarded by many as a guardian, not just as a defender. First, if all goes well she will be Pence's running mate, then when he has had two terms take up her father's mantle and do the next two terms in office. The Republicans are beginning to get it and the Democrats fear it, and one final note about Trump's second term: he could well be instrumental in bringing true peace to the Middle East. Watch this space and let's hope democracy wins.

Whoop whoop, I said it first.

One final thing (PS), I have not said why Margaret Thatcher is one of the five. What people did not realise was she knew the value of checks and balances and knew she had to bring order to her country: restore checks and return the balance. She followed all the rules of important decisions and came up with the secret ballot for union strike decision, paid for by the government. Epic, what a move, top girl. I was a union official for nearly half of my working life. The power that gave to all union members and unions was outstanding. No longer could bullying union leaders with their henchmen bring the country to its knees without a proper mandate from its members, thus saving this country. Well done, Maggie, you fooled them all: rest in peace with a smile on your face. May your God be with you.

The next section is a piece I wrote at the end of my fire service career. I am not going to put it as a chapter, but it is very relevant to this book: it is self-explanatory. Some of the pricing is out of date as it was written about 17 years ago; whilst it is a work of fiction it is factually based, read on.

OK
THIS WAS FIRST PUBLISHED SOME TIME AGO, I HAVE SINCE RETIRED BUT THE CUTS AND CHANGES STILL GO ON TO THIS DAY
THE FATE OF THE FIRE AND RESCUE SERVICE IN GREAT BRITAIN

PART 1

INTRODUCTION

When I first started this letter I only envisaged writing two or three pages but as you can see it has developed into quite a long essay. Please read it in its entirety. It has taken me several weeks to get it right. The views I express are my own, and while I don't wish to be derogatory, if I upset you with my views then all I ask is that you ask yourself: why?

I have been a firefighter with the SURREY FIRE AND RESCUE SERVICE (S.F. &. R.S.) for 30 years, as a firefighter for 14 years, and as a leading firefighter for the last 16. I joined the service in 1974 when I was 19 years old and I plan to retire in July 2005. I have seen many changes, been through two industrial disputes and I feel now that what is happening to our service does not bode well. Not only for those who deliver the service, but also for those who receive the service, the general public. This is causing me to put

Predictive analysis and the theory of consequence   99

pen to paper and express those concerns.

Some may find this very unpalatable reading. But I have nothing to lose and no axe to grind and I will be as factual as possible: something has to be said before lives are lost.

THE HISTORY LESSON

History has shown that politicians have long memories and when a group of people like, say, the miners cause them a great many problems, as they did with the Conservatives in the 1970s, it brought down the Edward Heath government. When next time that group raise their heads above the parapet the politicians will be ready for them, and for good or bad for all! That group will suffer the consequences but the politicians will not be seen to lose a second time and will exact their revenge.

We went on strike, quite justly so, for better pay and conditions for firefighters in the winter of 1977 and after a bitter, 9-week dispute the Labour Party were forced to sign a contract, giving the service a pay formula and conditions that could not be touched unless both sides saw a need for change and went into new negotiations or by act of parliament. And this was to last till 2002.

1978 was not a happy year for both the government and the country as a whole, seeing severe industrial unrest in both the public and private sectors. All of which culminated in a general election in 1979 and the Labour Party losing power for 17 years.

At this point I would like to give a small fact. In 1974 the life expectancy for a firefighter on retirement was, on average, five years. When you bear in mind that most retired early on ill health grounds or at the latest 55, very few saw their 60th birthday. Things have improved slightly but life expectancy is still only seven to ten years depending on which part of the country we serve. At the last count six firefighters who joined the job with me in 1974 are now dead.

PRESENT DAY

In 2002 it was recognised by both our employers and union alike that the pay formula was not working, the firefighters' skill base had grown beyond all recognition since 1977, and pay parity with skill base was such that retention of skilled staff was reaching crisis point in all areas, with London and the south-east of the country suffering the most staff shortages etc. Yes, I will hear you say, thousands of people apply for the fire service each year, but very few find they reach the standards required both physically and mentally, even though some of the physical standards have been reduced over the years.

Something had to be done and so both the union and the employers took the decision to go into negotiations over a new pay formula and conditions of service. So our old pay and conditions were now dead and the fate of our service was in the hands of our employers and the union (small note here for all that do not know: our employers are local government, not parliament).

Little did we realise what was about to happen next.

Early 2002 saw the employers and the unions agree that the skill base and risk levels needed to be rewarded, and an interim payment of 16% was agreed subject to government help and agreement, due to the fact that local government could not fund this rise without parliament's backing and funding. This was just, as it turned out, the right time for the Labour Party to seek revenge for 1977 and it was not a battle they could afford to lose or all the public services would be motivated to seek proper pay levels, compared to private industry, as they did in 1978 and the subsequent 17-year banishment of power for the Labour Party.

Prescott gave a flat refusal to the employers and even in June 2002 the alarm bells were not ringing for the union and we did not realise the trap we were all walking into. There was an independent report about the fire service conditions pay and fire cover due to come out which had been commissioned approximately two years before. There were interim findings. That is where the original 16% came from because the report had looked at pay parity with skill levels and recommended that firefighters' pay be increased by 40%. Also it was realised there needed to be an increase in fire and rescue cover and increases in spending in many areas.

The Labour Party completely ignored this report but realised they needed to make a counter-attack and announced they would be commissioning their own "independent" enquiry (at this point I am going to swear as I feel it is grammatically needed). Like bollocks it was going to be independent! With a four-month deadline, all those on the enquiry being appointed by the Labour government, with the leader announcing before the start of the enquiry on public television that the firefighters were not going to be happy with the outcome. Yeah right, this is going to be independent. Even our union knew what a farce it was going to be and took the view that the only course of action was not to participate, as there would be no point, but either way the union was onto a loser with the Labour spin doctors getting up and ready to malign and debase the service and the union at every level. The rest is history.

During the long and damaging dispute, control of the media by the Labour Party was quite apparent (in fact only Stalin and Hitler have had better propaganda machines), and in the end it was the deciding factor in its outcome. What with the militant union and the greedy, uncaring firefighters, who are a close kin if not in league with terrorists, and many other types of demonising rhetoric spewing forth from our papers, televisions and politicians.

'So who lost?' I may hear you ask.

We all have.

Plain and simply put, modernisation means CUTS. There are: less firefighters, less fire appliances, downgrading of services in Surrey alone with lots more to come and this is multiplied all over the country. In the past the only people to fight cuts in life-saving services are the union and the firefighters, but we now do not have the stomach for the fight because we have lost the belief in ourselves and we know this government have all the aces. They care little about your life; it's all about element of risk. One or two extra fire deaths are acceptable, who is going to notice? The 1947 Fire Services Act protecting your service has been torn up and discarded. They can do what they like.

Here I make a chilling prediction. The Surrey Fire and Rescue Service are going to lose one or more likely two firefighters in a back draught in the not-too-distant future, most likely at night and more than likely in the Haselmere or maybe the Walton area. Here are two scenarios. The first being before the cuts pre-2004, the second with what will happen now post-2004.

SCENARIO #1: PRE-2004

At 0030 hrs due to the happy reveller falling asleep, whilst his chips cook in his safely protected fire detector home on the outskirts of Haselmere, with his wife and three kids asleep upstairs, the chip pan reaches ignition temperature and ignites. Within seconds the flames are leaping to the ceiling and a few minutes later Fred is awoken from his deep slumber by the smoke detectors' high-pitched bleeping. He is immediately panicked by the smoke and

Predictive analysis and the theory of consequence

hears the baby crying who has also been woken by the smoke detector.

Fred rushes headlong up the smoke-filling stairs and crashes through his bedroom door. The twins, both girls, are now awake and frightened. There is a funny, unpleasant smell in their room and a haze reflected in the glow of their night light.

Fred has thrown his confused and frightened wife out of bed. He is shouting at her, "Get out! The house is on fire. Get out. Call the fire brigade I'll get the kids!" She quickly comes to her wits and grasps the cordless phone from beside the bed and rushes downstairs in the now thickening smoke, choking and spluttering. She was always good at texting and, even blinded by the fumes, before she hits the front door and stumbles into the fresh air she has dialled 999.

The first call, to 42 Beechwood Drive, was received by Surrey Fire and Rescue service at 0037hrs. The Fire Control Officer who took the call heard a woman coughing and being sick but she did catch the words "fire" and "Haselmere" and immediately the alerter was sounding at Haselmere fire station and a partial address was obtained before the phone went dead. Thankfully the full address is obtained from an automatic system and at 0038 both Haselmere's full-time pump S251 is alerted and mobile at 0039, and the retained pump crew is alerted S252 and mobile at 0044.

Fred bangs on the girls' door as he passes it, but realises he can't get them and the baby out at the same time. Sara and Sally cry out and Fred shouts at them to stay in their room and not move. The girls are confused and very frightened and start to cry, but they are good girls and do as their dad says. Meanwhile, Fred crashes into the baby's bedroom, scoops the baby boy out of his cot and heads for the stairs. As he passes the girls' room he shouts out,

"Girls! Stay there, I will be back in a second!" He is now terrified and panicked and choking on the ever-thickening black smoke, but with superhuman strength leaps down the stairs in one bound and is through the front door. He rushes up to his wife who is on the phone. He thrusts the baby into her arms, sending the phone crashing to the ground. They look at each other, eyes wide, and without having to say a word as both their minds are screaming, "THE GIRLS!" Fred turns and rushes back through the front door, back into the toxic smoke.

Alison grabs the phone from the ground and starts screaming as she realises the phone is broken. Mrs Smith from next door, who is a light sleeper, has popped her head out of the bedroom window and sees Alison. Realising Fred and Alison's house is on fire and the rest of the family must still be inside, she dives back into the bedroom, runs downstairs and dials 999.

Fred has bounded up the stairs holding his breath but he trips and smashes his head on the little vase table in the corner and falls back, momentarily unconscious, coming to at the bottom of the stairs. He has been lucky not to sustain any real injury, but his eyes are full of blood and he took a large gulp of smoke at the head of the stairs and stumbles back out of the doorway retching and choking.

Alison is hysterical when she sees her husband. He is black from the smoke and his face is covered in blood. "Where are the girls, Fred? Where are the girls?" Just at that point, the siren from Haselmere's wholetime fire appliance S251 wails in the distance. Fred comes to and looks at his wife. "They're in their bedroom. The door's shut." The siren is getting louder all the time. "The firemen will be here in a minute, they will be ok." Alison drops to the ground, sobbing, and rocks back and forth with her baby son held tightly in her arms. Lights are on in the surrounding houses; people are looking out of windows and standing in doorways, too afraid to move. They all know the family, they are good people. Some realise the girls are not with Alison and Fred and are horrified, glued to the spot: they can all hear the fire engine approaching. "Thank God the fire brigade were quick. This is awful", "Poor things", "I do hope the girls are ok".

Just at that point S251 turns into Beechwood Drive at 0045hrs, coming to a halt outside no 42 and the five-man crew jump out. Fred runs up to the officer in charge.

The second call to the S F & R S was received at 0041 and S251 was informed 'persons reported' the sub-officer immediately puts the sirens on and they stay on till they reach no 42 Beachwood Drive at 0045hrs. On arrival the scene is utter panic with smoke issuing from the front door. A smoky, bloody and panicked-faced man runs up to the sub-officer and grabs him by the arm, but it takes only seconds for the sub-officer to obtain the information needed. The two-man breathing apparatus crew are dispatched upstairs with a hose reel jet to the middle bedroom to rescue the two five-year-old girls, Sara and Sally, whilst the fifth man kneels down at the front door and pulses the second hose reel down the hallway towards the kitchen.

Sara has run over to Sally's bed and they are cuddling each other under the covers. They are good girls and love their dad unconditionally as only five-year-olds can and know he will come to their rescue. They have stopped crying but are still very frightened and their eyes are smarting from the smoke. Then they hear a noise and both pop their heads out of the covers. The bedroom door opens and smoke billows into the room. The girls scream at the two monsters, which loom out of the gloom. On hearing the little girls' wails, the monsters grab one each and head for the door.

Sara and Sally are rescued at 0049 hrs; both girls had fainted when grabbed by the BA crew but quickly recovered in the fresh air and, wide-eyed, they see the two monsters disappearing back into the house. Minutes later another fire engine draws up and two more not so scary men don their monster masks and follow the other firemen into the burning building. The fire at no 42 Beachwood Drive was brought under control at 0109 hrs. It takes several hours before the last fire appliance leaves the scene. This time this family were lucky. A SMOKE DETECTOR SAVED THEIR LIVES.

SCENARIO #2: WHAT WILL HAPPEN TODAY?

At 0030 hrs due to the happy reveller falling asleep, whilst his chips cook in his safely protected fire detector home on the outskirts of Haselmere, with his wife and three kids asleep upstairs, the chip pan reaches ignition temperature and ignites. Within seconds the flames are leaping to the ceiling and a few minutes later Fred is awoken from his deep slumber by the smoke detectors' high-pitched bleeping. He is immediately panicked by the smoke and hears the baby crying who has also been woken by the smoke detector.

Fred rushes headlong up the smoke-filling stairs and crashes through his bedroom door. The twins, both girls, are now awake and frightened. There is a funny, unpleasant smell in their room and haze reflected in the glow of their night light.

Fred has thrown his confused and frightened wife out of bed. He is shouting at her, "Get out! The house is on fire. Get out. Call the fire brigade I'll get the kids." She quickly comes to her wits and grasps the cordless phone from beside the bed and rushes downstairs in the now thickening smoke, choking and spluttering. She was always good at texting and, even blinded by the fumes, before she hits the front door and stumbles into the fresh air she has dialled 999.

The first call was received by Surrey Fire and Rescue Service at 0037hrs. The fire control officer who took the call heard a woman coughing and being sick but she did catch the words "fire" and "Haselmere" and immediately the alerter was sounding at Haselmere fire station and a partial address was obtained before the phone went dead. The full address is obtained from an automatic system. It's Saturday night and Haselmere's two pump-retained units have had a busy week. It's the height of summer and both pumps have had a busy few days and nights with grass fires etc. But as it has rained heavily during the day it will be a pretty safe bet that tonight will be quiet so only one retained pump is available for fire calls till 0900hrs. Haselmere's retained alerters were activated at 0038 for the crew to man S251. Sally is an experienced Fire Control Officer and this did not sound like a normal run-of-the-mill abandon call. She is a local girl and knows the area where the call came from and can't recall having suspicious calls from there before. In an instant she puts the bells down at Guildford, the nearest whole time unit, and turns out S221 just in case, which books mobile at 0040.

Fred bangs on the girls' door as he passes it, but realises he can't get them and the baby out at the same time. Sara and Sally cry out and Fred shouts at them to stay in their room and not move. The girls are confused and very frightened and start to cry, but they are good girls and do as their dad says. Meanwhile, Fred crashes into the baby's bedroom, scoops the baby boy out of his cot and heads for the stairs. As he passes the girls' room he shouts out, "Girls! Stay there, I will be back in a second!" He is now terrified and panicked and choking on the ever-thickening black smoke but with superhuman strength leaps down the stairs in one bound and is through the front door. He rushes up to his wife who is on the phone. He thrusts the baby into her arms, sending the phone crashing to the ground. They look at each other, eyes wide, and without having to say a word as both their minds are screaming, "THE GIRLS!" Fred turns and rushes back through the front door, back into the toxic smoke.

Chertsey lost their second pump in the cuts and at 0015 had an automatic fire alarm at St. Peter's Hospital Chertsey so S331 (Chertsey) & S292 (Woking's second pump) were still in attendance at 0037.

At 0030 S291 (Woking's first pump) and S222 (Guildford's second pump) are mobilised to RTC persons trapped. And both are in attendance at 0037.

The second call to 42 Beechwood Drive was received at 0041 and Sally quickly estimates that the fire is 'persons reported' she informs S221 and then calls up S251. There is no answer. Sally looks up to one of her fellow Fire Control operators.

"John?"

"Yes, Sally?"

"Can you ring Hazelmere retained and see if they are mobile yet? If they are at station can you tell them it is persons reported."

"Yes ok, Sally, I'm on it."

Sally then turns out one pump from Godalming retained at 0044 who book mobile at 0050. There are more and more repeat calls coming in, with some callers sounding very agitated. She can hear screaming in the background so she now informs the duty officer for the Haselmere area of the situation. He immediately books mobile but it won't be till 0109hrs before his arrival at no 42 Beachwood Drive.

Alison grabs the phone from the ground and starts screaming as she realises the phone is broken. Mrs Smith from next door, who is a light sleeper, has popped her head out of the bedroom window and sees Alison. She realises Fred and Alison's house is on fire and the rest of family must still be inside. She dives back into the bedroom and runs downstairs and dials 999.

Fred has bounded up the stairs holding his breath but he trips and smashes his head on the little vase table in the corner and falls back, momentarily unconscious. Coming to at the bottom of the stairs, he has been lucky not to sustain any real injury, but his eyes are full of blood and he took a large gulp of smoke at the head of the stairs. He stumbles back out of the doorway retching and choking.

Alison is hysterical when she sees her husband. He is black from the smoke and his face is covered in blood. "Where are the girls, Fred? Where are the girls?" "They're in their bedroom. The door's shut." "The firemen will be here in a minute, they will be ok." Alison drops to the ground, sobbing, and rocks back and forth with her baby son held tightly in her arms. Lights are on in the surrounding houses. People are looking out of windows and standing in doorways, too afraid to move. They all know the family, they are good people. Some realise the girls are not with Alison and Fred and are horrified and glued to the spot.

Sara has run over to Sally's bed and they are cuddling each other under the covers. They are good girls and love their dad unconditionally as only five-year-olds can and know he will come to their rescue. They have stopped crying but are still very frightened and their eyes are smarting from the smoke.

Alison looks up at her husband. He is clenching and unclenching his hands, standing as if rooted to the spot. Just then, Alison almost hesitantly says, "I broke the phone." Fred looks down. "What?" "I broke the phone." "Did you get through to the fire brigade?" She starts to cry. "I don't know," she weeps.

Fred looks horrified but grits his teeth. He remembers knocking the phone out of her hands when he thrust the baby into her arms; they both listen. They can't hear any sirens. They have been hearing them all week as Hazelmere has had a busy week fighting forest fires around the area.

Fred turns. "I am going to get our girls."

"O my God, Fred."

With this Fred turns and makes for the front door. This will be the last time Alison sees her husband. They would not allow her to see the body, it was too badly burnt.

Fred re-enters the house at 0045hrs. He moves slower this time, even though it only takes a few seconds to reach the top of the stairs. He is blinded by the acrid smoke and heat, his lungs are burning and he is choking on the toxic fumes. He becomes completely disorientated and, without realising it, he enters their main bedroom; his feet become entangled with the bedding, which had been dislodged earlier, and he trips and falls to the ground. He manages to struggle to his feet but he has taken in far too much smoke and collapses again. Just before he lapses into unconsciousness his last thought is: "Please, God, save my little girls. Please, God, save my little girls."

The driver of S221 is one of the safest and fastest Guildford has and tonight the appliance was flying. As luck would have it, the driver also used to live in Beechwood Drive so he knows exactly where the fire was. At 0056 the mobile phone on S221 rings. Pete the sub-officer picks it up. "Hello, Control." "Hello, Pete." "Is that you, Sally?" "Yes, Pete. Look, I thought I had better warn you, you are going to be the first pump there. The driver of S251 put his car into a ditch and he has had to run into the station about three miles as he had to pop round to his mother's. Anyway, we have had loads of calls to this incident and the situation sounds very bad, so I have also mobilised Godalming's second pump: they shouldn't be far behind you. There are two little girls and a husband trapped in the fire: the situation sounds very bad."

"Shit! Oh sorry, Sally."

"No, that's ok, Pete, I was thinking the same thing myself. Look, good luck and be careful."

"Ok, thanks, Sally."

Pete turns to his crew and informs them of the situation and what they might need to do on arrival. The driver grips the wheel with momentary fury. "Bloody modernisation! I'll give them modernisation. I'll stick it where the sun don't shine." He then bends back to the task in hand. He is now driving like a man possessed.

Pete feels a chill run down his back. He is more than unhappy. Instead of having a five-man crew, he is down to four. Just for a few quid travelling, they could have had five. Painshill were riding six tonight as well; sometimes penny-pinching can just go too far. But he keeps his thoughts to himself and looks ahead. They will be there soon enough. My God, we are going fast.

It's now 0049 and Alison has been standing since her husband had re-entered the house. Clutching the baby in one arm with her free hand over her mouth, she can't hold it back any longer. She is frantic as she starts screaming, "FRED! FRED! O MY GOD, FRED!" This is now all too much and the friends and neighbours come running. One takes the crying baby, which enables Alison to move closer to the doorway. Some friends pull her back but she tries to fight them off. She is inconsolable. "We have called the Fire Service, dear." One grumbles, "So did I, ages ago. They are only five minutes down the road. Call them again, John: you got your mobile on you?" So John, who is now angry and frightened, phones the Surrey Fire and Rescue Service at 0052. His is the tenth repeat call to the fire at 42 Beechwood Drive; meanwhile, Alison is still screaming out her husband's and children's names.

S221 book in attendance at 42 Beechwood Drive at 0001 they have made very good time from Guildford.

The mob fall back and there are murmurings of "About bloody time." Alison frantically runs forward to the fireman. The two BA men run out the hose reel to the front door. Paul puts the pump in and they check the hose is charged with water. Paul then runs over. He has recognised Alison, as he knew her at school. Pete is having a little trouble with her, finding out where the rest of the family are, she is so distraught.

"Pete, I know this girl and I know these houses. They have a closed-in stairway. If they're upstairs they may have a chance."

With this Alison calms. She is very close to collapsing.

He turns to Alison. "Alison, it's Paul. Where are they? Where are the kids?"

Alison looks up. "Fred, he went to get them. He went in ages ago. He said they were in the bedroom, their door was shut."

Calmly BUT firmly Pete asks, "Which bedroom, Alison?"

"The middle one." With this Pete and Paul look at each other and nod. There's a chance. The two BA men have heard all this and are already donning their breathing apparatus masks. They move to the doorway; Pete grabs the hose reel and turns to the two firefighters, as Paul leads Alison away.

"Listen to me, you two. If the father is on the stairway, bring him out but don't search for him, he'll almost certainly be dead. Get to the middle room. If the door is still shut there may be a chance the girls are still alive." Pete handed them the hose reel. They both shake their heads. "We'll travel faster without it." They all look at

Predictive analysis and the theory of consequence

each other. "I will pulse down the hallway, you two get in and out as fast as you can." The two BA men nod and enter at 0106.

Pete kneels down in the doorway with his visor down and pulses a spray of water towards the kitchen, up into the hot smoke. Paul runs back with the two BA wearers, tallies to set up the BA board and sees some fire appliances and an officer's car all turning into 42 Beechwood Drive.

At 0108 and 58 seconds the kitchen window finally gave way, letting the now fully pyrolysed kitchen breath. The back draught sent a ball of flame down the hallway and a pressure wave up the stairs. As it had been a chilly evening because of the rain early that day, the windows up in the main bedroom had just been drawn to, but not put on the latch. The pressure wave of the first back draught pushed open the two windows, letting in fresh air for nearly 40 minutes. The hot, highly flammable smoke had been filling the whole of the upstairs, and at 0109 the main, much more powerful back draught occurred, killing all inside the house. The top-floor windows were all blown out, throwing glass and debris all over the street with balls of flames reaching over 50 feet sideways. Thankfully no one else lost their lives that night but there were many minor and some major injuries sustained by both the general public and fire service personnel alike. Some people, mind you, will have mental scares they never will recover from.

Eventually, when the fire was extinguished, five charred bodies were found. The two firefighters, each still clutching the bodies of five-year-old Sara and Sally, and Fred, their father. IT'S NOT JUST ABOUT SMOKE DETECTORS. LOOK AT THE BIG PICTURE.

All of the people in these two stories are made up from my own imagination, and as far as I know there is no 42 Beechwood Drive in Haselmere, and this incident has never occurred. But everything else is as close to the facts as it can be and drawn from my experience as a firefighter of over 30 years.

Any alarm system is only as good as the backup systems in place ready to answer or cope with the emergency.

There is such a thing in law as a duty of care, and the 1947 Fire Services Act made sure a duty of care had to be adhered to by law. To change fire cover, remove fire appliances or to downgrade service meant consultation and justification regardless of costs. It also meant people could protest and stop downgrading. But the Labour Party saw this as a nuisance, so regardless of duty of care scraped the 1947 Fire Services Act. This left all at the mercy of vengeful politicians pressurising our employers and fire service management to make swathing cuts in all the Fire and Rescue services all over the country. We are being steam-rollered into a second-rate service, placing all in peril. The buzzwords are risk management: want to know what that is? They look at an area's fire deaths and if there is deemed to be a low risk, then a downgrade in service is required and once you lose your fire engine it isn't coming back.

It was said that to fund our full-pay claim and to keep the high level of service we all enjoyed before 2004, meant every council taxpayer paying an extra 1 penny per week in their council tax. Were we given a choice? No, of course not. It wasn't about the money, it was about vengeance. To scrap such an important bit of legislation without first proposing a better replacement was downright irresponsible, if not criminal. Yes, it was not perfect and did not reflect the amount of life-saving work carried out at road accidents, or the advances in fire-fighting technology. And it would have meant an all-party agreement, a good five years' worth of study and consultation before it was ready, although some of the groundwork had already been done on the first independent report on the fire service. No, not good enough for this Labour government. Their houses have not burnt down; their conference hotel has not been blown up. They have not had to be cut out of either of their two Jags after a road accident. Sorry, I am ranting now but I think you get my point.

In health and safety there is such a thing as safe practice. Is it safe practice to have four firefighters instead of five on a fire appliance? No, it's not. Is it safe practice only sending one fire appliance to any automatic fire alarm, property fire call or road accident? No, it's not. Is it safe practice not to send any appliance to automatic fire alarms unless it's a confirmed fire or a high-life risk, e.g. a hospital? No, it's not. Delayed response or minimum attendance is bad practice and inviting potential disaster. The only thing that will change what is happening now will be the losing of life. The question is: how many lives will be lost before then?

Everything costs money. A high-quality service, respected and recognised as one of the best all over the world, costs money. Leaving properties to burn to the ground costs money. Fire insurance costs money. Replacing all your worldly goods after fire costs money. Stopping a small fire in its early stages costs money. Saving lives costs money. Cutting people out of cars costs money. Rescuing people from disasters all costs money. Pay peanuts, get monkeys. Buy cheap and you get second-rate goods. Leave your services in the hands of irresponsible politicians and it will disappear until it costs more not to do something than to react.

SUGGESTED SOLUTIONS
First, a complete and comprehensive review of the service needs to be undertaken involving all parties. A strategy for the whole

country needs to be worked out. Big, long-term savings and a better emergency cover could be obtained. We all know that, if government and all parties made the commitment and investment.

Smoke detectors are not the only answer. Incorporate domestic sprinkler systems into the equation and now we are able to spread emergency cover over a wider area. The system only requires plastic piping from your water tank going to one or two sprinkler heads in each room. They are cheap to purchase and install, require little or no maintenance, are not reliant on electricity mains or battery, and as long as you have water in your water tank, you have a fire suppression system for life. And it will only cost between £1000 and £1500 for the average, three-bed family home. They are only suppression systems, but have proved in the United States that they will put out most domestic fires. Fire-fighting appliances can cover larger areas where whole towns have adopted the system, but it does mean an initial investment. Long-term, however, insurance cover will be cheaper, less fire damage, and along with smoke detectors more lives will be saved even if fire cover is reduced.

WHAT CAN WE DO?

Well, the pen is mightier than the sword. On the first page you will see all the people and organisations I have sent this essay to. Please feel free to copy this report and send it to anyone who you think needs to see it, and if you can put a note in from yourself with why they might need to read it, then all the better.

Also if you feel like myself, even if you don't agree with some of the things I have said, please put pen to paper and send a short or long note to all the people I have sent this essay to. One brick in a pond only makes a ripple; a whole stack makes a large wave. Tip lorry loads in and the banks flood. Something may then get done.

Predictive analysis and the theory of consequence

My address care of Chertsey fire station is also provided. I would love to get some feedback so if you could send me a copy of your response as well, I would appreciate it.

Lastly I would like to say on a personal note I am proud of what I have achieved in my years in the service and I know that I have been involved with the saving of hundreds of lives as a team with my fellow firefighters at fires and road accidents etc. I am proud of my fellow colleagues, the commitment, courage and sacrifices they have all made in the pursuit of their duties. And lastly I am proud of the service and despite the last two years would I do it all over again? Yes, I would.

Thank you for you time to read this AND IF YOU WANT TO RESPOND THEN PRINT THIS OFF SEND IT TO YOUR MP AND YOUR LOCAL COUNCILLOR OR ANYONE ELSE YOU FEEL NEEDS TO READ IT, BECAUSE EVEN IF YOU DON'T LIVE IN SURREY YOUR FIRE SERVICE IS BEING CUT.

It is now 26/8/20: we are at war, we are going to win. But I need to qualify the last bit about the last two years of my service. I only say this because as a defender for so long it finally took its toll emotionally and if I had not been blessed with such a good watch I might not have made it; it might have beaten me. I am very glad it did not. Whilst some of them could be fuckwits sometimes, when it mattered they were all fantastic firefighters when they needed to be, and were the best watch I served with. I have to give a special mention to two of them. First of all my last officer in charge: he transferred into Surrey from Wiltshire, was younger with only half the time in. But I respect the rank and the person, nothing else. He was the best officer I ever served with. Unfortunately he died with, I believe, a brain aneurism whilst on duty. May your God be with you and losing to you at chess, everyone misses you. And finally to Alison the best driver I ever had. She transferred in from London and was brill. One day we were discussing the merits of driving skills, Alison was just sitting there taking it all in, like she did, not saying much, but with a slight smile on her face when one of the guys had a fwit moment and said to me, "Well, who do you think is the best driver on the watch, then?" "No-brainer, Alison of course. If I had my way she would be my driver every time I was officer in charge of the appliance." Jaws dropped. Alison smiled and said it how it was; the boys could not argue, she was right and she was my driver every time I was in charge after that. Damn, she was good; shame about the Easter bunny, though, lmao another story. Any of you guys reading this, I am still very proud to have served with you all, you got me through. Thank you from the bottom of my heart.

Andy Allwood

Truly this is the last thing.

The pigs were getting fed up with all this meat they were being fed: 'experts', nasty fwits and crazed politicians. It was not the fact that they were hard to catch and screaming, they were well aware of their fate if the vegans came to power. The exercise will mean they can keep lean and mean, and the screaming, well, it just sharpens their hearing. So not only will they hear the vegans coming, but if they manage to get in they will be able to outrun the pasty bunch. It's the bitterness they are beginning to get tired of, the bitter taste. Why can't they just cook a few? The dogs reckon that makes them far tastier. "Still, bacon being regarded as one of Andy's five a day, all is forgiven, matey." "Ok throw in another, we are hungry."

CHAPTER 19:

SURPRISE! THIS IS THE LAST PAGE OF MY BOOK. Well, nearly anyway.

First of all, if you are one of those people that have to read the last page of any book you buy as you go down the page, you will stop, get your money out and have to buy it to answer my questions.

If you are reading the last page because you were intrigued with what was on the cover about the last page, same. Oh get your money out, sucker (no, you will enjoy it).

If you are reading it because you are a fwit* (*see introduction), let me tell you now, you can't put it down and walk away because the shop assistant has seen you look and read the last page and knows, because they have read the book, that you are a fwit if you put it down and walk out. Get your money out. (But you will enjoy it and probably redeem yourself from being a fwit and help change the world: whoop, whoop.)

As you have bought and read my book, here are some questions for you:

1. Did you enjoy my book?
2. Did it make you laugh?
3. Did it make you think?
4. Did it make you sad or even cry?
5. Are you now, or already, making small steps?
6. Would you recommend my book to a friend?
7. Would you keep it and read it again (and not give it to your

friend because they can afford to buy it)?

If the answer is yes to at least four questions, then I am thrilled. If the answer is yes to five or all of them, I am super-thrilled and it is an international bestseller and I am able to convert my D2 2.5-ltr Tdi Land Rover.

Thank you very much, may your God go with you. Until next time, keep you and yours safe.

Andy Allwood

THE END

What comes next?
ATTACKERS, DEFENDERS AND CANNON FODDER
SECOND BOOK IN THE COVID WAR SERIES

Cannon fodder, attackers, defenders

You can take the girl out of the trailer park, but you can't take the trailer park out of the girl.

A leopard cannot change its spots (I am going to have fun trying to disprove this one, buckle up).

And a question on your lips: "Surely Stalin was a nasty fwit." God, no, he was a very nasty fwit, let me explain. (This is going to be fun.)